BRIGHT LAND

Lois Darroch

BRIGHT LAND

A WARM LOOK AT ARTHUR LISMER

Introduction by Walter Klinkhoff

MERRITT PUBLISHING COMPANY LIMITED
Toronto/Vancouver

Canadian Cataloguing in Publication Data

Darroch, Lois, 1912–
Bright land

Bibliography
Includes index.
ISBN 0-920886-07-8 (trade ed.)

1. Lismer, Arthur, 1885–1969. 2. Painters – Canada –
Biography. I. Title.
ND249.L5D37   759.11   C81-094809-5

Published by Merritt Publishing Company Limited
Toronto/Vancouver
Distributed in Canada by John Wiley and Sons Canada Limited

To CRISTINE and JOHN UNIACKE BAYLY

JENNIFER, MELISSA and TIMOTHY

Contents

List of Illustrations

Preface

The writing of BRIGHT LAND: *A Warm Look at Arthur Lismer* has been a pleasure from the beginning. Almost without exception the response to my queries from those who remember Lismer was smiles, happy reminiscences, and praise of him as artist, teacher and human being.

I cannot explicitly remember my first knowledge of the work of Lismer and the Group of Seven. Like Canada itself they seemed always to have been there as part of my heritage. Unaware at the time that they constituted a controversy in the art world, I simply enjoyed Lismer's *Bright Land*, MacDonald's *A Tangled Garden* and Harris's *North Shore, Lake Superior*.

The idea of writing a biography of Lismer came to me after the completion of my biography, *Robert Gourlay, Gadfly: Forerunner of the Rebellion in Upper Canada 1837*. Through curious circumstances I happened to view *Belgian Refugees* and a sketchbook pertaining to the Thornhill and Halifax periods of Lismer's life. They revealed an aspect that I had not associated with the artist of the well-known landscape paintings. My writing pen and artistic sense were sufficiently piqued that I began the research that has resulted in this consideration of Lismer's life.

The treatment herein is narrative rather than analytical. It is possible that I should have probed more deeply into the motives that underlay changes in his choice of painting subjects that led to the Montreal still lifes and the semi-abstraction of some of the East Coast seaside subjects. As they were nowhere clearly stated, it did not seem proper to conjecture – and that may be just the way Lismer would have wanted it.

LOIS E. DARROCH
Toronto, 1981

Acknowledgments

No work of this nature can be written without the assistance, large or small, of many people.

My first and greatest debt is to Marjorie Lismer Bridges for supplying hitherto unpublished family pictures and for checking dates and facts with the same generosity of spirit that characterized her father.

I thank also those former associates of Arthur Lismer's who shared with me their memories – Dorothy Drever, Helen Frye, Tillie Cowan, Phyllis Hipwell Janes, Norah McCullough, Erma Lennox Sutcliffe, Naomi Jackson Groves, R.M. McLean, Charles Goldhamer, Harold Beament and the late Donald Mackay.

Special thanks for valuable assistance are accorded Doris Heustis Mills Speirs and Alan Collier.

I am grateful to archivist Hunter Bishop and the executive of the Arts and Letters Club for their generous help.

Cheerful help was rendered by the staffs of the National Gallery of Canada, the Art Gallery of Ontario, the Metropolitan Toronto Library Board, the McMichael Canadian Collection, the Montreal Museum of Fine Arts, the Edmonton Art Gallery, the Dalhousie University Art Gallery, the Art Gallery of Hamilton, the Norman MacKenzie Art Gallery, Rodman Hall Arts Centre, the Agnes Etherington Arts Centre, the Canadian War Museum and other public galleries and institutions whose pictures have been credited here.

Invaluable was the kind and generous assistance of Karen Keenlyside Mills, Walter Klinkhoff, Neil Kernaghan and Noel Saltmarche, who made it possible to see many fine Lismer works in private collections. I only wish we could have included more of them in *Bright Land*.

My thanks are extended as well to the commercial galleries, corporations and individuals who own Lismer paintings and drawings, for allowing them to be photographed.

To all who gave me their assistance my heartfelt thanks, and apologies for any inadvertent errors.

L.E.D.

Introduction

One of the greatest pleasures of my career as an art dealer is the opportunity to meet people of the quality of Arthur Lismer. I first met Dr Lismer in 1950, when much of his career lay behind him. Although our relationship remained professional (Lismer kept his private life very private indeed), we met often. Dr Lismer's office at the Montreal Museum of Fine Arts was only a short walk from my gallery. I found him delightful – kind and generous, with a warm and spontaneous sense of humour. Lismer's work had always attracted me, and personal acquaintance with him deepened my understanding and appreciation of his work.

There is a prevalent critical tendency to regard the early work of many artists as their best. This attitude persists in spite of the fact that history is full of artists who reached their creative peak late in life. (Titian, for example, painted his greatest masterpiece at the age of ninety-nine!) Those who identify Lismer solely as a member of the Group of Seven tend to view his later work, which departs from the popular and easily recognizable "Group" style, as evidence of deterioration rather than a positive artistic development.

For many years Lismer painted Group of Seven subjects – islands, hills, lakes and forests, usually viewed from a distance – rendered in his own distinctive style. By the time the Group disbanded he had tired of these and turned to new images and themes. While continuing to draw his inspiration from nature, Lismer moved closer to his subjects. Painting from this new, more intimate perspective made a significant stylistic difference: his work now had a definite abstract quality to it without actually being generically abstract. It is this aspect of his later work which has been misunderstood and unjustly maligned. To change one's style and outlook late in life is an act of personal courage and imagination: the later work of Arthur Lismer deserves re-appraisal.

Always joking, invariably kind and courteous, Lismer never said anything critical about another human being, especially another artist. One of those people who always do more for you than you can do for them, his generosity was constantly in evidence. Parents of his students would often find a work of Lismer's that they had admired handed to them casually as a gift. They would bring it to my gallery, pleased but somewhat unaware of the value of the gift and the generosity of the giver.

It is perhaps unnecessary to assert Lismer's importance in the history of Canadian art. As a founding member of the Group of Seven and as the creator of paintings that constitute a significant and lasting contribution to our culture, his status is secure. In his long career as a teacher he inspired two generations of students, leaving a lasting impression on all who were fortunate enough to come in contact with him. Arthur Lismer's name is held in the highest regard and his reputation, deservedly as great as that of any other Canadian artist, will continue to grow.

WALTER KLINKHOFF
Montreal, 1981

Lismer's last two pictures gave me a feeling of exhilaration and joy. All his works are fine, but he is going on to higher and bigger things, sweep and rhythm of the lines, stronger colours, simpler forms. He was extremely nice.... He is lecturing now, spreading the gladness of the newer way, revealing the big, grand things of this country to its sons and daughters.... Oh, God, what I have seen? Where have I been? Something has spoken to the very soul of me, wonderful, mighty, not of this world. Chords way down in my being have been touched.... Oh, these men, this Group of Seven, what have they created? – a world stripped of earthiness, shorn of fretting details, purged, purified; a naked soul, pure and unashamed; lovely spaces filled with wonderful serenity. What language do they speak, those silent, awe-filled spaces? I do not know. Wait and listen; you shall hear by and by.

EMILY CARR, 1927
Hundreds and Thousands
upon meeting Arthur Lismer for the first time

Figure 1
King and Yonge Streets, Toronto
C.1911

CHAPTER ONE

The Beginnings of an Artist

As a country that has been formed by immigrants, Canada is constantly receiving surprises from the people who come to her shores. One of the happiest occurred in early 1911, when Edward VII was king of England and the sun never set on the British Empire; the Liberal prime minister of Canada, Sir Wilfrid Laurier, would soon lose an election over the issue of reciprocity; and a move toward the avant-garde in art was imminent.

In Toronto, the city for which Arthur Lismer was headed, those ensconced as residents had a name for fresh immigrants from England. It was "bronc," short for bronco, meaning one not yet broken in to the pace that the city had established for itself. Lismer, an artist from Sheffield, Yorkshire, was "the damdest [sic] bronc you ever saw."[1] In a few years his astonishing mental and physical energy would help make him one of the founders, one of the mentors, and the comic relief of the revolutionary Canadian art movement known as the Group of Seven.

Canada was not exactly ready for an artistic shot in the arm. Her tastes strongly favoured little girls in fields of daisies or sombre Dutch representations of fields, trees, and ponds in which cows seemed to stand perpetually immobilized. Lismer joked that for years he thought European artists painted them in puddles because they didn't know how to paint cows' feet. When he and his Canadian friends began to exhibit, one critic complained that their art looked like a plesiosaurus in a fit because it deviated from the conventional norm.

Canada was not alone in North America in her scorn for innovation in art. Just a few years before the work of the emerging Canadian artists would be assailed, Alfred Stieglitz, dean of the most advanced art movements in New York, was writing to Gertrude Stein in Paris: "...there is no feeling for art, or love for art, in the United States yet. It is still considered a great luxury...and all this in spite of the so-called interest in old masters and the millions spent for them."[2]

When Arthur Lismer arrived in North America from Sheffield, he was already well acquainted with the old masters, and well trained with brush and pencil. Born on June 27, 1885, he seemed always to have had a restless drawing hand. He was always settling down in the house at 7 Raven Road to sketch and daub. His father was a draper's buyer, and the family lived respectably in a modest but attractive section of Sheffield, well away from the "Works" to the east where cutlery and other articles were manufactured. When Lismer was thirteen, he read in the local newspaper that the South Riding County authorities were offering scholarships to young artists at the

Figure 2
7 Raven Road,
Sheffield, England

Figure 3
Edward and Harriet Lismer,
Arthur's parents

Sheffield School of Art. With no prompting at all he applied, sat for the three-hour Saturday-morning examination, and was one of twelve who received scholarships. It meant free evening tuition for seven years.

The uncertain life of an artist has rarely appealed to parents as a proper vocation for their offspring, and Lismer's parents were no exception. They could not help acknowledging his obvious talent, but felt that he must have some means of earning his living. He was soon apprenticed to a photo-engraving firm, Willis Eadon & Co.

Those were the days before quick commercial photography. Subjects to be photographed were still required to "watch the birdie" as they remained motionless in front of the cameraman hidden under his black cloth. Newspapers therefore employed artists to make quick sketches on the spot. Part of young Lismer's training as an apprentice was to make sketches for the Sheffield *Independent*. He was soon sketching such speakers as prickly George Bernard Shaw, cocky Winston Churchill and Pankhurst suffragette and theosophist Annie Besant. This newspaper work introduced him to the ideas expounded by budding activists and allowed him to indulge a flair for carica-ture. It also taught him speed in sketching. He said later, "All those years of sketching were the most important of my train-ing. Young artists don't sketch enough. They want to start in with paints right away."[3]

Lismer could rarely be found without a sketchbook in his pocket. He was soon adept at quick sketches that captured, in a few expressive lines, the personality of his subjects. Sometimes the feeling evinced by the sketchbooks indicated that he was impatient with the restraint imposed on him by his classes. The classroom figures are cut sternly to the scale of the page and the profiles are traced with a heavy pencil. Yet sometimes his pencil seemed possessed of a spirit of its own. He drew his painting companions with loose, rollicking lines quite different from those that comprised the staider portraits. Once in a while a caricature burst forth. Lismer may have accepted the rigour of his training at the Sheffield School of Art, but his sketches showed that he would likely tread a path of his own.

The city of Sheffield that was providing this basic training

Figure 4
The Heeley Art Club

Figure 5
Arthur Lismer and his sister Constance

was industrial in nature but not entirely devoid of feeling for art. It took artists and skilled craftsmen to create the designs and supply the expertise that went into industrial products. Engraving itself was an art so highly regarded that the Royal Academy elected engravers to its hallowed midst. The brother-in-law of an aunt of Lismer's, Thomas Barlow, who had been articled to a firm of Manchester engravers at the age of fifteen, had been elected an associate of the Royal Academy in 1873 and a full member in 1881. He had engraved the work of Turner, Millais, and Phillips. Barlow died when Lismer was four, but stories of the London art world flickered in family conversations for years afterward whenever these relatives came to visit.

Mere talk about art, weekday apprenticeship work and haphazard sketching were not enough to satisfy this young fellow's urge to create. In his mid-teens Lismer joined the Heeley Art Club, a club for amateurs that had been founded in 1895. The Heeley Art Club was a vigorous society that held regular working and criticism sessions, weekend sketching excursions and shows. Its members were mostly local businessmen who met in the Meersbrook Vestry Hall. When dressed in their Sunday best for a picture, the members presented a solid and dedicated front.

On their weekend excursions, young Lismer's long legs (he

Figures 6 – 10
*Sketches from the artist's
Sheffield period.*

was over six feet tall) could outmatch any of them in seeking a spot to paint, and soon he was accepted by the more prestigious Sheffield Society of Artists. At the age of eighteen he hung his first canvas in an exhibition of that group. It was a landscape painting and, though he loved the thrill of swift pencil or ink sketching for the newspapers, it was landscape painting that was his passion. For years Lismer had collected reproductions of the works of John Constable, who, almost a century before, had turned from the subjects of antiquity popular in his time to paint the unspoiled nature that he loved. To achieve the effect that he sought he had abandoned the subordination of colour to line that Academicians were united in praising, and began to apply his colour in quick, short strokes, sometimes even with a palette knife. Colour, not line, produced form, distance and depth. This method revealed the strokes of the brush rather than concealing them as the old masters had done. Constable's work could in many ways be considered the forerunner of Impressionism that was the fashion of Lismer's day.

With the influence of friends like Frederick Varley, who had returned from studying at Antwerp's Académie Royale des Beaux Arts, it was no surprise that Lismer decided to take advantage of the free tuition there. He was twenty-one and had finished his apprenticeship and scholarship work, categorizing them both with youthful arrogance as stultifying but necessary. When he was invited to share the home of George Gale, a teacher in a Berlitz language school, he pocketed his savings and set out for Belgium in September 1906.

He lived with the Gales at first and rented a studio over a baker's shop, spending six hours a day at the same exacting Académie where Vincent van Gogh had studied in 1885. The rest of the time was spent painting on his own or absorbing the life of a city that had a museum containing original Rubens and other old masters. He took side trips to Paris where Picasso had just painted *Les Demoiselles d'Avignon*, and visited the actual scenes in France that had inspired Corot and Daubigny. He felt the pull of the Fauves – artists such as Matisse, Rouault, Braque and Derain, who had erupted onto the art scene in France in 1905 with their free use of colour extravagantly applied in pure pigment. He was deeply stirred by French

6

7

8

9

Impressionism with its gay and pearly tints, even though the French government, when offered sixty-five Impressionist paintings, nearly refused them on the grounds that "For the government to accept such filth there would have to be a great moral slackening."[4]

For a year and a half Lismer lived in the exhilarating atmosphere of the continent where art was taking on new forms. Then it was time for this man of twenty-two to earn his living, to return to Sheffield to open a business in the downtown Haymarket Chambers as a photo-engraver. It was a struggle to make the business pay enough for his own livelihood, and he soon had a compelling reason for wanting more. His eye and his heart had been caught by Esther Mawson, sister of one of the members of the Heeley Art Club. In 1908 they became engaged, but Sheffield could not provide enough work so that they could afford to marry.

Lismer had a friend, William Broadhead, who had gone to Canada where he had found employment as a commercial artist. If other emigrants were doing so well, why couldn't he? Lismer consulted his fiancée and family. They were reluctant to agree but supported him in his decision to move to Canada.

Toward the end of 1910, Arthur Lismer took one last fling at

10

the art world of Europe. He traveled to London to see an exhibition of French Post-Impressionist art organized by art critic Roger Fry at the Grafton Galleries. Here were paintings of Gauguin, Lautrec, and Lismer's admired van Gogh. It was here that he first viewed the works of Cézanne, who toward the end of his career was painting richly, intensely, almost wildly. Here were the modern rebels, all together in one glorious outbreak of colour. It was a wonderful send-off for an artist-emigrant.

In January 1911, Arthur Lismer sold his business, made a trunk out of his wooden desk, and sought new fields to conquer and to paint. He left Liverpool on the s.s. *Corsican* and arrived in Halifax nine days later in the midst of a driving blizzard. He traveled steerage, and landed with five dollars in his pocket. "I don't recall it with any particular pleasure," he said during a radio broadcast,[5] but the next day, with his friend Broadhead's help, he had a job as a commercial artist in a lithographing plant on Church Street in Toronto.

While he traveled from Halifax to Toronto by train, Lismer observed the great expansive snow-clad country with his landscape-painter's eye. "Who is painting this vast country?" he wondered, as he gazed at mile after frozen mile.[6] When he

Figure 11
*Arthur Lismer's farewell card
from the Heeley Art Club*

changed jobs a month after his arrival to work at the Rapid Grip and Batten Company, a commercial art firm familiarly known as "the Grip," he was soon to find out. His co-workers and their friends were painting this country and they were ready to look at it with fresh, non-European eyes. Not for them just cows in puddles.

Freshness often goes unappreciated. These were the very men who would soon have their paintings described as resembling the contents of a drunkard's stomach. Had Arthur Lismer landed on his feet in this new country or dived into a snake pit?

NOTES

1 J.E.H. MacDonald to F.B. Housser, December 20, 1926, in the possession of Thoreau MacDonald
2 John Brinnin. *The Third Rose*. Boston: Little, Brown & Co., 1959, p. 176
3 Gail Scott. Amherst *Daily News & Sentinel*, April 26, 1968
4 Sarah Newmeyer. *Enjoying Modern Art*. New York: Mentor Books, 1957, p. 60
5 "Voice of the Pioneer," CBC radio broadcast, March–April 1964
6 Undelivered interview for CBC radio, c. 1964

Figure 12
A view of Georgian Bay

CHAPTER TWO

The Impact of Georgian Bay

The Rapid Grip and Batten Company itself was no snake pit. It was a leading design and engraving firm, with the highest standards of any commercial art firm in Toronto. Its art head, Albert Robson, was as exacting as any teacher Arthur Lismer had ever had at the Sheffield School of Art, and he also had a talent for attracting some of the best men in the field – senior illustrators J.E.H. MacDonald, Lismer's Sheffield friend William Broadhead, Tom McLean, Stanley Kemp, Frank Carmichael and Tom Thomson. Among these individuals there prevailed a remarkable spirit of helpfulness and camaraderie, instead of the jealousy that often pervaded similar establishments. They accepted the bronc immediately.

With this job and these friends Lismer not only had an income, but he was in the midst of the art world of Toronto. Toronto, unlike the then more affluent Montreal, made no distinction between artists working in the commercial field and those few with the good fortune to be exclusively creative artists.

In the spring of 1911 Lismer was invited to exhibit with the Ontario Society of Artists. As he viewed the show with his Grip friends, it was not their pictures that made the greatest impression on him; it was a painting by a young Montreal man. A.Y. Jackson's *At the Edge of the Maple Wood* depicted a farmhouse yard in Sweetsburg, Quebec. The yard, edged with a snake fence, was soft with spring run-off and the tree branches, ready to bud, cast intricate shadows. It was so real that one could almost smell the wet, warming, revivifying earth. This picture, said Lismer later, "stood out among the usual pictorial array of collie dogs, peonies and official portraits like a glowing flame packed with energy and loveliness. I can remember looking at it with MacDonald, Thomson and Harris and talking enthusiastically about its quality."[1]

It moved them deeply, particularly the bronc. He recalled later:

I was a newcomer, raw English, full of enthusiasm for new scenes but finding Canadians just a little strange and lacking in imagination, humour and refinement.

I *was* raw. I confess it, but I knew what this country was like. I'd been in it at least two months; then I saw this Jackson canvas in 1911 and when one has been living for twenty-five years in England one sees only English arts... . I did not know a single Canadian work, except MacDonald's and then Jackson's – these raised my spirits and changed my views.... Jackson's *Maple Wood* created a feeling of settlement and permanency [in me] about a land of which my first impressions were impermanent and transient.[2]

Figure 13
Albert Robson, art director at
"The Grip"

This painting, he wrote later, was almost an historic document in Canadian art.

Lismer's next insight into Canadian painting came with a Toronto exhibition of Quebec artist Maurice Cullen. Cullen, like Jackson, had studied in Paris where he was greatly attracted by the work of the Impressionists. On his return to Canada he adapted their method to the Canadian landscape, particularly snow scenes. Great painter as he was, there were no buyers for his new style. Once he auctioned off one hundred of his paintings in one fell swoop, averaging eight dollars a canvas. When Lismer saw Cullen's works he was "struck by their quality and valid interpretation of the Canadian landscape and the way in which the artists had combined in them the Impressionist mode with a Canadian spirit."[3]

A restlessness was beginning to seize the Grip group, a desire to develop their own style of painting instead of following the accepted mode. MacDonald in particular was beginning to talk about a national school of landscape painting, of creating a Canadian tradition in art even though the idea was current that traditions could exist only in Europe. One of MacDonald's friends who shared his vision was Lawren Harris.

There was no need for Lawren Harris to work at the Grip or anywhere else. He had an independent income as a scion of the Massey Harris farm implement company. No dilettante, however, he had studied art abroad and had exhibited with the Ontario Society of Artists that same year, 1911. Harris was also a member of the Arts and Letters Club of Toronto, as was Tom McLean of the Grip who soon invited Lismer to join. This was another red-letter event for the newcomer.

The Arts and Letters Club was unique in Canada, for it was the first to be formed of an amalgam of members from the various arts – painting, writing, music and drama. Founded in 1908, its membership included men active in the arts and such patrons as banker Byron (later Sir Edmund) Walker, founder of the Champlain Society and co-founder of the Art Gallery of Toronto and the Royal Ontario Museum. Arts and Letters members met at lunches which, in their first quarters in a third-floor garret, were toted up two flights of stairs from a restaurant opposite the King Edward Hotel. By the time Lismer joined, the Club had moved to the old Assize Court Room behind No. 1 Police Station on Adelaide Street. To get to the great room with its enormous fireplace, members picked their way past the manure pile produced by the police horses. The facilities of the room offset the malodorous entrance. It was large enough for the presentation of plays, musicales and the boar's head procession that accompanied the festive Christmas banquet. In less than a year of arriving in Canada the youthful Lismer had been accepted into Toronto's most prestigious group of creative men.

Members of the Arts and Letters Club mingled easily, but often the artists sat together at the "Artists' Table." Whenever Lismer lunched there, laughter erupted continuously, either because of the cartoon sketches he could throw off as easily as he cut a slice of bread, or from the outrageous quips that bubbled from him just as readily. Once, undaunted by the gold watches and chains that adorned the vests of some of those about him, he took a large, cheap watch from his pocket and proceeded to wind it noisily during a lull in the conversation. Lawren Harris was present. As Lismer persisted in his winding, someone called out, "Where did you get that old Massey Harris?" "Oh, from Time, the grim Reaper," he quipped instantly.[4]

Between Club lunches he returned to his work of turning out ads for Eaton's catalogues or similar commissions. Once, after drawing a set of perfectly pressed underwear he had to let off steam. He drew another picture that gave the Long Johns a living personality – they looked as if the wearer had not taken them off since the previous November.

To fill the gap left by his break with the Heeley and Sheffield art societies, Lismer went sketching around Toronto on weekends with his new friends. One result was *The Banks of the Don*, painted in a style reminiscent of Constable. The picture was sylvan, silent, subdued. Only a few bright splashes of blue indicated that the brilliant Canadian sunshine had induced him to paint the sky differently from the luminous English and Belgian skies that he had once lived under.

So he worked, joked at lunch at the Arts and Letters Club, painted, and longed for the day when he would have saved enough money to marry. By the spring of 1912, a year and a half after he had come to Canada he had four hundred dollars,

Figure 14
306 *Delaware Avenue, Toronto*

Figure 15
THE BANKS OF THE DON
*c.*1912
oil on panel
13.7 × 22 *cm*

enough to return to England to fetch Esther. After their wedding and a honeymoon in Belgium, they rented a house in Toronto at 306 Delaware Avenue.

At this uncertain moment Arthur Lismer dared to leave his commercial art work and salary at the Grip to go freelance. His friend Jim MacDonald had done so the previous year and one of the results was *Tracks and Traffic*. It was Impressionist in style, though it did not imitate the peculiar dream-like quality of Impressionism that made walking figures seem to float in the air. MacDonald's figures were firmly rooted – in the snow. The painting attracted favourable attention when it was hung in the OSA spring exhibition at the St George Street public library. The following year Lismer's contribution, *The Clearing*, painted one Sunday afternoon on an outing with Tom Thomson, was also well received.

A.Y. Jackson, painting in Montreal but soon to be associated with the Toronto group, was not so fortunate. Montreal still preferred Dutch women peeling potatoes in dark interiors or sheep eating their way across pastures. Jackson and R.S. Hewton had closed their joint exhibition in the spring of 1913, unnoticed and unsold. They would not be unnoticed for long; they were vilified after the next exhibition of the Art Association of Montreal. The Montreal *Witness* headlined: "Post-Impressionists Shock Local Art Lovers at the Spring Exhibition – Screaming Colours and Weird Drawing Cause Much Derisive Comment." And the Montreal *Star's* critic, S. Morgan-Powell, assailed these moderns: "Post-Impressionism is a fad – an inartistic fetish for the amusement of bad draughtsmanship, incompetent colourists, and others who find themselves unqualified to paint pictures."[5]

Jackson's feelings were assuaged when he received a letter from Jim MacDonald in Toronto asking him if he still owned *At the Edge of the Maple Wood*. If so, his friend Lawren Harris would like to buy it. Harris had been unable to forget the painting and decided to take the plunge of patronizing an unknown Canadian artist. This request brought Jackson to the Arts and Letters Club in Toronto where he finally met MacDonald (with whom he had only corresponded), Harris, Lismer, and Fred Varley, whom Lismer had persuaded to come to Canada from Sheffield.

One sale seemed to precipitate others. When Tom Thomson's *Northern Lake* was bought by the Ontario government, he cashed the cheque in one-dollar bills. In May Arthur Lismer bounced home on the College streetcar to announce, three days before the birth of his daughter Marjorie, that the government had also bought *The Clearing*. With his cheque he bought a crib and carriage for the baby.

Equally propitious for the artists was the news that Lawren Harris and another Arts and Letters Club member, Dr James MacCallum, an ophthalmologist with a strong interest in Canadian art, had begun to build the Studio Building on Severn Street near the Rosedale Ravine. The Studio would rent reasonably to artists who lived in houses too small to provide adequate painting space and light. The building was three storeys high with northern light, and offered six large studios with eighteen-foot ceilings where big pictures could be painted and small sketches worked up to adequate size. It was a home for the artists.

Dr MacCallum had features that resembled those of the Dutch burghers whose portraits and cows the younger Canadian artists were seeking to supplant, but he too was dissatisfied with the long-standing emphasis in Canada on Dutch art. He owned a summer cottage *Westwind* on an island in Georgian Bay. Because Muskoka was becoming too populated for their tastes he and a group of University of Toronto professors had purchased a tract of land that they sub-divided among themselves. In 1913 the Georgian Bay area was north country to most Torontonians who had never been farther from home than the villages in southwestern Ontario where their grandparents had been born. MacCallum loved the north, and he was on the lookout for artists who would depict it as he felt it should be painted. In 1912 he invited Jim MacDonald to stay in a houseboat near his cottage and paint. The following summer MacDonald went to Mattawa to paint and the Lismer family was invited to occupy Dr MacCallum's cottage after he had returned to the city in September.

At this time, Lismer's painting was competent as evidenced by the sale of *The Clearing*, but he needed fresh scenes to spur him on, and he was not one to refuse an adventure. Esther Lismer, though reared in a Bedfordshire village, was a good

Figure 16
Dr James MacCallum c.1915

enough sport to journey with her husband and four-month-old baby to a cottage on an island. They traveled by train to Honey Harbour and then by boat around Beausoleil Island over the deep-coloured September water to MacCallum's cottage.

Only one who has been freshly introduced to Georgian Bay, not raised beside it, can appreciate the impact of that glorious landscape on a newcomer. It is like being on a different continent – the radiant air, the rocks, the endless expanse of turbulent water and sky, the magnificent sturdy stance of pine trees pitted against the wind, only a hundred miles from rolling, elm-embroidered, maple-rounded southern Ontario. It was a Canada Lismer never dreamed could exist. He was shaken by the revelation of the new and wonderful landscape. "Georgian Bay!" he wrote, "thousands of islands, little and big, some of them mere rocks just breaking the surface of the Bay – others with great, high rocks tumbled in confused masses and crowned with leaning pines, turned away in ragged disarray from the west wind, presenting a strange pattern against the sky and water....Georgian Bay – the happy isles, all different, but bound together in a common unity of form, colour and design. It is a paradise for painters."[6]

Moved as he was by the new experience, two weeks were not enough for him to absorb its feeling completely and adapt his style to cope with it. He returned to his freelancing in the city and painting up his sketches in the Studio Building that Mac-Callum and Harris had now finished. Here he completed, among others, *Georgian Bay* (1913), with its Impressionistic, summer-coloured sweep of sky. A few islands were dwarfed by sky and water instead of being rife with the strength of the rock that comprised them. There was nothing of the solidity of the land, the force of the water or the pervasive presence of the pine trees. His paint, however, was becoming thicker, less Barbizonian in interpretation, but Corot and Constable were still too close to him. No painting technique he had ever practised in Europe could cope with Canada.

Another member of Lismer's group of friends was becoming successful at portraying the landscape. When the Lismers left Dr MacCallum's cottage in mid-September, Alex Jackson was invited to move in and he stayed until winter. He returned with

Figure 17
GEORGIAN BAY ISLANDS
*c.*1921
pencil on paper
28.8 × 39.7 *cm*

paintings that were different from those of Morrice, Cullen and Cruikshank, different from Lawren Harris's houses in central Toronto and MacDonald's *Tracks and Traffic*, different even from his own *At the Edge of the Maple Wood*. That autumn he brought back the sketch that, working in the spacious Studio Building, he would enlarge into his first big painting. *Terre Sauvage* (Wild Land), was deep and powerful in colour, strong in subject, and the beginning of a new interpretation of the northern Canadian landscape.

Jackson also brought back with him enough paintings for an exhibition at the Arts and Letters Club in December. These did not escape the pen of a critic at the "Critics' Table" (which Lismer dubbed the "Knockers' Table") in the Arts and Letters Club. The Montreal comments about Jackson's painting in the 1911 spring exhibition paled in comparison to the words of the Toronto *Star* critic, H.F. Gadsby, who hissed that Jackson and all the younger artists who displayed a modicum of the same trend were like "Advanced Atomizers who spray a tube of paint at a canvas and call it 'Sunshine on the Cowshed' or words to that effect.… the net result being more like a gargle or gob of porridge than a work of art." He called them "The Hot Mush School," and described their work as "a plesiosaurus in a fit…or a hob-nailed liver."[7]

Other critics were more complimentary, but Gadsby's "Hot Mush School" appellation was hard to live down. Jim MacDonald answered him heatedly in the same paper on December 20th: "Let us support our distinctly Native art, if only for the sake of experiment." The group of Toronto friends, which now included Jackson, was about to engage in a Cause, the Cause of painting Canadian, not European.

This little contretemps in Canada was mild in comparison with what had taken place months earlier south of the border as the newest art from Europe reached the United States. This art had left even the Impressionists behind. On February 13, 1913 the epochal Armory Show, the first comprehensive international exhibition of modern art in America, had opened in New York and then moved on to Chicago where enraged art students and the Law and Order League attacked it both verbally and physically. When the show moved to Boston a woman, fainting at the sight of a cubist painting, fell against Raymond

Plate 1
THE CANAL AT
DONCASTER 1906
watercolour over graphite on
wove paper
30 × 46 cm

Plate 2
GEORGIAN BAY 1913
oil on canvas
71.8 × 92.1 cm

Duchamp-Villon's bust of Baudelaire and smashed it. The Armory Show brought to the United States a little of the whirlwind that had seized modern art since the later works of Cézanne.[8] One wonders whether Gadsby would have been driven insane if he had been there.

Opposition to Jackson's work produced a certain exhilaration among the friends of the attacked. Gadsby's criticism put them in the world league. Toronto was too insular and unsure of itself to consider it a compliment that its artists were progressive. Not too remarkably, since five of these painting friends – Jackson, Harris, Carmichael, Varley and Lismer – had studied in Europe, a spin-off from this international whirlwind was gathering slowly and starting to blow over Canada. It was the Georgian Bay country that had set it in motion.

NOTES

1 John A.B. McLeish. *September Gale: A Study of Arthur Lismer.* Toronto: J.M. Dent and Sons Ltd., 1955, p. 44
2 Arthur Lismer. "A.Y. Jackson, LL.D., Painter of Canada: An Appreciation," January 30, 1942, (speech in manuscript), Art Gallery of Toronto
3 Joan Murray. *Impressionism in Canada: 1895 to 1935.* Toronto: Art Gallery of Ontario, 1974, p. 132
4 Harold Beament to Lois Darroch, March 20, 1976
5 F.B. Housser. *A Canadian Art Movement.* Toronto: Macmillan Company, 1926, p. 71
6 Marjorie Lismer Bridges. *A Border of Beauty.* Toronto: Red Rock Publishing Company Limited, 1977, p. 28
7 H.F. Gadsby. Toronto *Star*, December 12, 1913
8 John Brinnin. *The Third Rose.* Boston: Little, Brown & Co., 1959, p. 176

Figure 18
Algonquin Park

CHAPTER THREE

Algonquin Park and Thornhill

If Arthur Lismer had been moved beyond measure by his introduction to Georgian Bay, he had yet to experience untamed Algonquin Park, where lake after lake could be reached only by portage, and the trees came so close to the water's edge that no shore line was visible. For over a year he had heard Tom Thomson's and Bill Broadhead's enthusiastic reports of the unspoiled wilderness of the park. Thomson had traveled there for the first time in the spring of 1912 and later that summer had canoed with Broadhead from the park to Spanish River and Lake Huron.

Before his contacts with his colleagues at the Grip, Thomson had rarely painted more than was required for his work in advertising layouts. Now, inspired by his friends, he had begun to paint with an intuition for nature that was almost miraculous. His better-trained artist friends could give him pointers on the use of brush and paint, but no one needed to guide him in his perception of the spirit of the land. He was a man who was at home with the wild.

Thomson's descriptions of Algonquin Park fired the imagination of A.Y. Jackson as well. After his return from Georgian Bay, Jackson spent from February to April of 1914 in the park and was joined for a time by J.E.H. MacDonald and J.W. Beatty. That spring Thomson left Rous and Mann Press Limited, the company to which the Grip group (except for Lismer) had moved two years before, and worked free-lance like MacDonald, Lismer and Jackson. Again he went to the park to paint and this time Lismer joined him, traveling the nine-hour train journey from Toronto. Here Canada revealed to Lismer another facet of her scenic riches:

Spring in the Park...is one of the wonders of God's creations.... We were there just after the ice had gone out of the lakes and before it had completely gone from the southern slopes of the shores of the lakes. We were there before the maple and birch burst into leaf, and we stayed to see the wonderful miracle of a northern spring come again; we were there when the first spring flower came up, and bravely faced the frosty nights and chilly mornings, and we stayed to see the woods carpeted with their infinite variety of colour – the little white Canadian violet, the sweetest scented of them all. Trilliums, Hepaticas, Jack-in-the-Pulpit, auriculas, anemones, to name only a few.... We were there in a wonderful time when everything was on the very edge of re-birth.[1]

In England, Lismer had never sketched more than an hour or two away from the ubiquitous Sheffield pubs, or on the well-

Figure 19
Arthur Lismer

Figure 20
TOM THOMSON c.1914
pencil on cardboard
26.4 × 33.4 cm

populated English east coast. Even the previous summer on Georgian Bay he had used a rowboat to fetch the baby's milk and never been out of sight of habitation. He marvelled at the preparation necessary now before they disappeared for two weeks away from the ranger's quarters at Canoe Lake into the bush. From Canoe Lake they moved to Molly's Island in Smoke Lake where they set up their tent and from there visited Ragged, Wolf and Crown lakes.

Relatively self-taught Thomson who liked solitude and artistically trained, gregarious and witty Lismer were not always the most complementary companions. Thomson once told Jim MacDonald that sometimes Lismer made him nervous, for "Arthur's eyes are so sharp they bore right into me."[2] But Thomson could paddle a canoe while the inexperienced Lismer at first sat safely in the bottom. Thomson could cook over uncertain outdoor fires the simple fare they packed in with them. They were there to paint and everything else was secondary. There was nothing to disturb them as they absorbed the feeling of the park and struggled to transform it on canvas into something that satisfied.

The artist friends had had many conversations about the merits of Impressionism as a painting method. Lismer was going through a phase of experimenting with broken colour as a means of expressing the spirit of the park. In *The Guide's Home, Algonquin*, painted at the mouth of Potter and Joe creeks, the birch trees burgeoned in a bright spring haze of palest purple and green under the life-renewing sun and a cloudless sky. It was a highly successful picture, and the largest he had attempted. It is still one of the best Canadian examples of the transplanted technique of Impressionism. But no European method could begin to capture this country, no miniscule French pointillism, no quick, light Impressionistic dashes of colour. These were techniques suited to civilized beaches or cafés; they were powerless against the mounded rocks, the brown, lucent water and the strong green spruce and pine of the park.

Although Lismer had not succeeded entirely in capturing the total essence of the park, he wrote that "the thrilling days were turning points in my life."[3] Thomson had introduced his friends to this locality and they were excited over the experi-

Figure 21
THE GUIDE'S HOME,
ALGONQUIN 1914
oil on canvas
100.3 × 113 *cm*

ence. Once again, they were mutually helpful. Both Lismer and Jackson, from their European experience, had already given Thomson advice about painting techniques, but Thomson was maturing quickly. His friends were now learning from him to use magnificent pure colours in impasto to capture the verve of this country.

All too soon the bites of the infamous Canadian black flies drove them out of the deep bush. Lismer returned to Toronto to paint up his sketches in the Studio Building. Thomson remained in the park, and painted *Moonlight, Early Evening* which when exhibited at the OSA Spring Exhibition, was bought by the National Gallery.

The other focal point in Toronto for Lismer and his friends remained the Arts and Letters Club. Byron Walker was still a member and was now the chief trustee of the National Gallery. The new director of the Gallery, recently arrived from England, was the brilliant and perceptive Eric Brown. Taking a stand that aroused the disapproval of the conservative elements of the Royal Canadian Academy, both Walker and Brown actively encouraged the work of the younger painters. Through the shows at the Arts and Letters Club and the OSA

Figure 22
Eric Brown, first director of the
National Gallery of Canada

Figure 23
WOOD INTERIOR,
ALGONQUIN PARK 1914
oil on panel
23.2 × 31 *cm*

they kept watch over developments in Toronto. As often as he could, Lismer lunched at the Club where he continued to be a prime entertainer.

Again he sketched in and around Toronto. After his first visit to Algonquin Park he bought a 9- × 12-inch sketch box that held several panels, although he still used his larger 9- × 16-inch one. With the smaller size he could paint astonishingly fine miniatures. In *Autumn, Albion Hills* (1914), he reduced a great panorama into miniature, every detail of distance clear and technically magnificent. There was an oddity about it, however. The sky was brilliant, Canadian blue, but the hills and trees were Constable-brown. England was still in his palette. Another miniature, *Autumn Glory*, was a marvel of French Impressionism, a scene of great beauty, similar in colouring to *The Guide's Home* but small and delicate as a jewel. Although Lismer might be struggling still to capture the true feeling of the north country, there was no question about his competence.

In the summer of 1914 the Archduke Ferdinand of Austria was assassinated at Sarajevo and German jackboots marched through Belgium, scorning the treaty of Belgium's neutrality as only a scrap of paper. On August 4, 1914, Canada followed Britain in a declaration of war. The "war to end wars" had begun and the boys who went off cheering expected to be home by Christmas victorious and alive.

In the autumn, Lismer took Esther and two-year-old Marjorie to Algonquin Park. Again he sketched with Thomson who had remained in Algonquin Park all summer, painting and guiding. Jackson came up and so did Varley. From his spring trip Lismer had painted *Smoke Lake, Algonquin Park*, but he was still far behind Jackson and Thomson in both richness of composition and execution. He knew it. He wrote to his friend Dr MacCallum from Canoe Lake Station in October: "Jackson has some brilliant work, better than his Rockies' studies. The material here is more intimate and suits his aggressive soul better, I think. Varley and I are struggling to create something out of it all and hope to have something to show as a result of our efforts."[4] The four men together produced an explosion in enthusiasm and paint. Each could work separately but proximity reinforced their efforts and sparked their creative urges. More important, they were letting the country speak to them instead of imposing an academic painting method on the landscape.

There was scarcely time before winter set in to think about what they were doing, scarcely time to organize an approach to the scenes before them. Lismer wrote later: "The essence of nature's efforts is not permanence but change, and the sketcher must seize one eternal moment, decide what to do and put it down....he must first compose his ideas and then his mind, then his plan of attack, and finally the finished picture."[5] Right now there was little time for analysis, just feeling.

Then it was back to Toronto to work up sketches, both from the park and from the Georgian Bay trip of the year before. Lismer's work was becoming bolder in composition and colour, but it lacked the full strength of the locality; there was still no satisfying relationship between rock, water and sky, no stong unity, no real capturing of elemental forces.

The spring of 1915 brought another Ontario Society of Artists exhibition. The pictures of what was beginning to be called the Algonquin Park School stood out among the more conventional paintings of Robert Holmes, Wyly Grier and George Reid for their bolder use of colour and feeling for the

out-of-doors. Thomson entered his impressive *Northern River*, which the National Gallery bought. Jackson, MacDonald, Carmichael and Harris submitted winter scenes and Lismer showed *Sunlight and Shadow*. For him personally this picture was an advancement. There was a firmer movement of line and form, a surer grasp of subject.

Augustus Bridle of the Toronto *Star* praised their work, but Hector Charlesworth, art critic of *Saturday Night* magazine, assailed the obnoxious trend toward Impressionism in the paintings of the Algonquin Park School. Charlesworth was a member of the Arts and Letters Club who sat at the Knockers' Table, close to the Artists' Table. The verbal sallies that were sometimes exchanged between the two groups at the Club now became more than mere pleasantries. Lismer and Jackson in particular wanted people to accept their paintings for their own worth, not be damned by someone who wanted to judge them on a Procrustean bed of preconceived ideas. Their approach to art, the artists felt, was a tribute to the country, and as artists, not onlookers like Charlesworth, they were doing what they felt needed to be done. No one was going to stop them.

In March of 1915, Lismer again painted at Go Home Bay. Knowing that times were lean, for the disruption caused by the war was already beginning to make itself felt on the economy, and free-lance design commissions were scarce, Dr MacCallum commissioned murals for his cottage as a birthday present for his wife.

Thomson's contribution to the murals was a twisting, flat design in dull blue, tan and green. MacDonald painted traditional Canadian figures of an Indian, hunter, priest and courtier. Lismer put into his panels all the gaiety of cottage life – children on rocks, a woman standing in high-buttoned boots with her arms stretched to the wind, ducks flying high, and a large panel, "Skinny Dip," set against deep blue water and sky.

This was the year when Lismer decided to move to Thornhill, a village with a population of three hundred, about five miles north of Toronto. J.E.H. MacDonald had moved there two years before. MacDonald's wife's parents lived with him, and his wife was in poor health. Esther Lismer would help look after her in the large house at 121 Centre Street. When the

Figure 24
121 *Centre Street, Thornhill*

Figure 25
*Arthur Lismer with his wife
Esther and daughter Marjorie in
Algonquin Park*

weather was fine, Lismer entertained them all with his antics on the lawn.

MacDonald's fourteen-year-old son Thoreau, two-year-old Marjorie and an assortment of dogs completed the enlarged household. At varying times there were two Scotties, one called Garry and a mongrel called Boots. After a few months when a house became vacant at 5 John Street, the Lismers moved into their own home. Soon the two artist families were joined by Fred Varley and his family, and Frank Carmichael, newly married and fresh from a nine-month stint at the Beaux Arts in Antwerp. No blinding light of artistic inspiration had come to Carmichael in Europe, but on his return he worked doggedly, waiting for a breakthrough.

Lismer too waited for a breakthrough, but there was free-lance work to be solicited and the war was unsettling. Thomson gave *Afternoon, Algonquin Park* to the Canadian Patriotic Fund to sell. Lismer donated *Breezy Weather, Georgian Bay*. There were calls for posters to encourage enlistment and the purchase of victory bonds. Some of the posters went crudely to the point: "Yours not to do or die, Yours but to go and buy." MacDonald designed a poster showing a great eagle of war besieging an empty countryside while a woman in a hooded cloak mourned at one side. It was flatly patterned and impressive.

Lismer essayed the same theme, but his portrayal refused to

Plate 3
AUTUMN IN ALGONQUIN *n.d.*
oil on wood panel
20.4 × 26.4 cm

Plate 4
UNTITLED (*Belgian refugees*) 1915
gouache
45.7 × 58.4 *cm*

Plate 5
**SPRINGTIME ON THE
FARM** *C.*1917
oil on canvas
30.4 × 40.6 *cm*

Plate 6
POPPIES, BEDFORD PARK
AVENUE 1924
oil on board
66 × 81.3 *cm*

Figures 26–29
THE MACCALLUM
MURALS 1915–16
oil on beaverboard

26   27   28   29

Figures 30–31
THE MAC CALLUM
MURALS 1915–16
oil on beaverboard

30

31

become a poster design. He had lived in Belgium. He could see in his mind's eye the friends he had left behind. He could envision the roads jammed with fleeing, stricken women and children. What emerged from his brush was a moving depiction of refugees crowding in along a road with their bundles. A soldier assisted some people into a cart like a tumbril carrying them to an unknown fate. A priest administered last rites to one who had already succumbed. Through the trees and over a wayside cross streamed the rays of the sun – was it in sadness, benediction, or in mockery of man's inhumanity to man?

Other than the war, life in Thornhill was pleasant and pastoral. They lived quietly but productively. The highlights of this time were evenings spent talking with Jackson before he enlisted, and the brilliant, stimulating Harris. It was MacDonald who first had the dream of a new national school of painting, but Harris was a vigorous exponent and constant inspiration. Lismer was a catalyst. No gathering in which he took part could ever be dull.

So they painted, sought inspiration, and painted. Now the brushes of "the bunch," as MacDonald once called his lighthearted friends, were being affected by an element even newer than the Impressionism that had caused such an outcry. The design fashion of the day for commercial artists was art nouveau, a clear but convoluted form of decoration. When they went out painting now this trend was teaching them to wrestle into clarity the tangled, untouched nature of the wilder parts of Ontario that are so difficult to capture. They were learning to isolate some of the elements that nature spread lavishly before them just as they controlled and filled the space given in a commercial assignment. They were also learning to effect a picture with recognizable elements that still gave unity to the scene. Tom Thomson was about to paint *The Jack Pine* and *The West Wind*, applying intuitively his training in design to the untamed scenery of the north.

Oddly enough the next critical storm for these artists would not come from their portrayals of the north with its tremendous vitality. It would emanate from the innocuous garden at 121 Centre Street in Thornhill.

For a couple of summers Lismer had worked in the war

garden of the Arts and Letters Club in the valley at Hogg's Hollow near York Mills Road and Yonge Street. The Club had initiated the project partly as a way of increasing food production in war time and partly to provide cheap food for the Club table. In Thornhill the MacDonalds and the Lismers now had good-sized gardens of their own with fruit trees, vegetables and flowers. Here Lismer painted his pleasant *My Garden, Thornhill*, and MacDonald produced *The Tangled Garden*. MacDonald's painting represented vividly the autumnal profusion of a nature so prodigal that humans could not keep pace with it. The colours were brilliant, the mood insouciant. A large sunflower with bending head dominated the centre. MacDonald said that he intended it to be nodding jocularly to his friend Arthur Lismer.

MacDonald hung *The Tangled Garden* in the 1916 OSA spring show. Reaction was instant. A reviewer at the Toronto *Star* wrote about the exhibition: "There are some examples of that rough, splashy, meaningless, blatant, plastering and massing of unpleasant colours which seem to be a necessary evil in all Canadian art exhibitions now-a-days...all tinged with the same blustering spirit of post-impressionism... ."[6] Hector Charlesworth of *Saturday Night* went even further. Singling out *The Tangled Garden*, he inveighed against it "as an experimental picture that destroyed the effects of very meritorious and sincere pictures that are hung on the same walls." MacDonald, he claimed, was throwing his paint pots in the face of the public. He said that *The Tangled Garden* was a masterpiece compared with MacDonald's *The Elements* and *Rock and Maple*, which for all they really conveyed might just as well have been called "A Hungarian Goulash or Drunkard's Stomach." MacDonald's impulse, he continued, had also infected a number of other talented artists who seemed to think that crudity in colour and brushwork signified the qualities "strength and self-expression."[7]

Again it was the usually gentle MacDonald who answered those stinging words with a letter to the editor, "Bouquets from a Tangled Garden," that was printed prominently on the editorial page of the *Globe*. No statement could have been clearer:

One would think that if it is the function of the artist to see, the first duty of the critic is to understand what the artist saw.... A ribald and slashing condemnation without justifying analysis of any picture approved and hung by a committee of artists is rarely, if ever, necessary in the public interest.... *Tangled Garden, Elements*, and a host more, are but items in a big idea, the spirit of our native land. The artists hope to keep on striving to enlarge their own conception of that spirit... in a new country like ours, which is practically unexplored artistically, courageous experiment is not only legitimate but vital to the development of a living Canadian art.[8]

Lismer's *Westerly Gale, Georgian Bay* was not attacked in the same manner. It was complimented as having fine atmospheric qualities but this was the last Georgian Bay canvas that he would paint for some time. The world of the artists who only five short years ago had met at the Grip drawing tables was under more than the critics' attacks. Jackson had enlisted in 1915 when it became clear after the first battle of Ypres that the war would not be over by one Christmas or even two or three. He was wounded at Sanctuary Wood. Harris, mourning for a dead soldier brother, was at officers' training camp at Borden. MacDonald was busier now with War Records paintings than tangled gardens. Varley was still working for Rous and Mann prior to going to No Man's Land on a commission as a war artist.

Lismer, still free-lancing, had decided in 1915 to accept an offer to teach the six-week teachers' summer course given at the Ontario College of Art. His reputation as a painter was sufficiently strong to qualify him eminently for the position, and the money earned was cash in hand. Though steady work cut into his painting time, he found that he did not dislike it. In his off-hand, half-deprecatory fashion he said later, "I found I had the gift of the gab" (had anyone doubted it before?) and "some scrapings of intellect that prompted me to teach."[9]

His work in the 1915 and 1916 summer courses attracted attention to his prowess as a pedagogue, and in 1916 he was invited to become principal of the Victoria School of Art and Design in Halifax. He was guaranteed $1,000, acceptable for

Figure 32
Lawren Harris c.1917

the time and, as he remarked, it was enough to support a wife, a child and a dog. With the exception of MacDonald all his friends had scattered. The steady income would compensate him for the fact that Halifax as an art centre was not as advanced as Toronto.

Lismer's acceptance of the position was in part an acknowledgment that the life of a free-lancer was difficult, even though it gave him ample time to paint. It also meant that he enjoyed teaching and was confident that he could succeed as an administrator as well. No force on earth would have made him take the position if he had not thought he could make it a success, and it was with this challenge in mind that Lismer and his family moved to the east-coast port of Halifax late in September 1916.

NOTES

1 Unpublished manuscript in the possession of Marjorie Lismer Bridges
2 Thoreau MacDonald to Lois Darroch, 1978
3 John A.B. McLeish. *September Gale: A Study of Arthur Lismer.* Toronto: J.M. Dent and Sons Ltd., 1955, p. 48
4 Arthur Lismer to Dr James MacCallum, October 11, 1914, MacCallum Correspondence, National Gallery of Canada
5 Arthur Lismer. *Water Colour Painting for Pleasure.* Canadian Legion Educational Services series, no. 194, p. 12
6 F.B. Housser. *A Canadian Art Movement.* Toronto: Macmillan Company, 1926, p. 109
7 Hector Charlesworth. *Saturday Night.* March 18, 1916
8 Toronto *Globe*, March 27, 1916
9 "Voice of the Pioneer," CBC radio broadcast, March–April 1964

Figure 33
Patrol Boats, Dartmouth, Nova
Scotia 1917

CHAPTER FOUR

Halifax

In 1916, Halifax was a city of only 80,000, but again the Lismers chose to live in a nearby village location. They rented a three-bedroom house with an acre of land in Bedford, a suburb located ten miles from the city at the mouth of the Sackville River. As the rent was ten dollars a month and coal heating fairly inexpensive, Lismer's salary was adequate for comfortable living. Esther Lismer could walk down the hill to the Anglican church where the Red Cross meetings were held and khaki-coloured wool was knitted endlessly into socks and scarves for the boys overseas. Three-year-old Marjorie had plenty of space to play and the wooden trunk her father had brought from England made a good toybox. Lismer traveled daily by train to Halifax to his work at the Victoria School of Art and Design at the corner of George and Argyle streets (now the Nova Scotia College of Art and Design on Duke Street).

The school had been founded in 1887 by the indefatigable Anna (The King and I) Leonowens when she returned from Siam. It was the first government-supported art school in Nova Scotia. She had helped raise funds which enabled a school to be opened on the upper floor of Union Bank on Hollis Street. The premises soon proved to be too small for the unexpectedly large enrolment of two hundred and sixty-five.

The first principal, George Harvey, an English landscape painter, resigned in 1893 because of poor working conditions. Three other heads in the next three years tried unsuccessfully to cope. Under the fifth principal, Henry Rosenberg, a former student of Whistler, the board bought and remodelled the old National School facing the Grand Parade corner. Though the building was old and drafty, Haligonian Lewis E. Smith doubled the enrolment between 1910 and 1912. Numbers fell again under Lismer's immediate predecessor, the Frenchman Georges Chavignaud, a lover of water colours. When the teenaged students tired of watercolours, his main solution for their boredom was to set them boxing.

When Lismer arrived there was only a handful of pupils in the dilapidated building, and no extension program existed for either adults or children. There was no great enthusiasm for art in the city beleaguered by war, and the board of governors was not prepared for a man of Lismer's exuberance. The only bright spot in the situation was that they were determined to keep the school alive, even if they were not prepared to spend money to create a more viable situation.

The new principal began a publicity trip by making the rounds of the schools, using every facet of his "gift of the gab" to expound the delights of artistic endeavour. No one could be

Figure 34
Marjorie in front of house in Bedford, Nova Scotia

Figure 35
THE LITTLE DRIFTER AND
THE BIG FREIGHTER *c.*1919
lithograph
32.4 × 43.8 *cm*

more persuasive than he when he set his mind to it. In a few weeks he had three more pupils and a little later about twenty teenagers in Saturday morning classes. By the second year he had developed his own regular courses and a growing attendance in daytime classes. He also began a course for teachers.

Some of his pupils were servicemen stationed for varying lengths of time in Halifax, hungry to snatch what they could of normal life from the demands of their service existence. A young naval officer named Harold Beament came one day to see if he could participate in classes whenever his ship would be in port. Lismer gave him a plaster cast of a foot to draw, and satisfied with the reproduction he admitted the man to class. Before he could attend a single session Beament was ordered to another base of operations for the remainder of the war. Some years later at a Group of Seven exhibition in Toronto Beament walked over to the vice-principal of the Ontario College of Art asking admittance to a class. "Ho," snorted Lismer, "you're the fellow who sketched a foot for me in Halifax and then disappeared. Are you going to try that trick again?"[1] In the Second World War Harold Beament commanded an escort group of mine-sweepers in the Gulf of St Lawrence before being appointed a navy artist. He later became a major figure in Canadian art and Lismer's good friend.

Plate 7
THE RIVER DRIVERS, *n.d.*
oil on panel
22.9 × 39.5 *cm*

Plate 8
WINTER CAMOUFLAGE 1918
oil on canvas
71.1 × 91.4 cm

Lismer lost no opportunity to observe the drama of a war-time port both from the nearby Halifax docks themselves or from his home at Bedford overlooking the Basin. In the great Halifax harbour the battleships came and went, as did the tugs, tenders and mine-sweepers. On the docks were the sailors, the stevedores, the soldiers outbound, the Red Cross nurses with their flowing white head-dresses, the women trying not to weep as they waved goodbye or as they met the stretchers coming off the hospital ships.

Toward the north end of the harbour a passage called the Narrows led to the inner harbour named Bedford Basin, five miles long. Here ships gathered for a convoy to take them across the Atlantic. One evening the Lismers would see the Basin filled with ships and wake next morning to find it empty, the ships having departed soundlessly during the night.

On December 6, 1917, the year after the Lismers went to Halifax, a French ship, the *Mont Blanc*, loaded with 4,000 tons of TNT, 2,300 tons of picric acid, sixty-one tons of other explosives and a deck cargo of benzine, was proceeding to anchor in the Basin to wait for a convoy. A Belgian ship, the *Imo*, plainly lettered in red and highly visible, was leaving the Basin with a cargo of relief supplies for Belgium. In clear daylight the two ships collided in the Narrows.

The impact set the *Mont Blanc's* cargo ablaze, and the flames raced down a ventilator chute into the main cargo hold where the TNT was stored. The blast blew the ship to bits, and a huge mushroom-shaped cloud arose. For a few moments Halifax harbour was dry as a bone. Then the debris in the cloud came crashing down over the ships and city.

Ten miles away the Lismer family was sitting down to breakfast later than usual, for it was Arthur's day off in mid-week to compensate him for working Saturdays. They heard the gigantic roar, and the house trembled. The soot from the stovepipe sifted slowly down upon the dishes and white table-cloth, "It must be the furnace," Lismer exclaimed. "Get Marjorie out of the house while I see what it is."

There was nothing wrong with the furnace, but the fan light over the front door and several upstairs windows were broken. Then they saw a column of black smoke rising from the direction of the distant harbour. "I must go to see if the school is all

Figure 36

STERN OF A DEPARTING TRANSPORT 1917–18
lithograph
40.8 × 32.7 cm

right," said Lismer. He walked the ten miles into the city.

The biggest man-caused explosion in the history of the world until then had buried the train, which Lismer had not taken, under the collapsed station. Many of the commuters had been killed. The dead were everywhere, some in grotesque postures because of broken limbs, some without a mark, killed by concussion only. It was cold. Later in the day, snow drifted down to veil some of the horror.

Until the news spread by word of mouth, no one knew what had happened. Some thought it had been an earthquake, some that German zeppelins had bombed the city, others that submarines had torpedoed the harbour. No one could imagine that two ships could collide in day-time, particularly one loaded with explosives, which should have been proceeding with special care. The two ships were now gone and Pier 8 was annihilated. Trains were derailed. The north end of Halifax was blasted flat. Rescue workers began to put the dead in piles of ten, and when the final count was taken, 1,635 men, women and children had been killed, 6,000 were injured, 200,000 were homeless. Many had been blinded by flying glass.

There was no possibility that the art school had escaped damage. When Lismer entered his office, he discovered that a rolled window blind from the City Hall across the Parade had pierced the north window and was driven into a wall across the room. Windows were broken, blinds were torn, one dividing wall had collapsed and the pictures were flung everywhere. It was bad enough to find damage done to what the school owned, but Lismer felt responsible for two borrowed displays, an exhibition of lithographs from the National Gallery in Ottawa and one of small pictures by the Ontario Society of Artists. Upon examination he found that the damage to the pictures was less than he had expected. Only a few had been pierced by window glass, although most of the picture glass was broken. Eleven plaster casts were damaged. Before the school was cleared of debris it was used as an emergency centre, then filled with coffins, empty until the dead were identified. One of his best students was among those killed.

In spite of his horror at the sights that met his eyes, Lismer still retained the instincts of a newspaper artist that had been fostered during his apprenticeship in Sheffield. He did some quick sketches. Though he claimed that his first concern as an artist was landscape, there were few subjects that he could not draw with expertise. He sent four sketches to Gus Bridle, editor of the *Canadian Courier* in Toronto,[2] and some others to the Sheffield *Independent* that published them as coming from "our artist on the spot."

As soon as he could, he wrote to tell Eric Brown of the National Gallery that most of the Gallery's traveling exhibition was safe:

The devastated area is a terrible sight and those who know say that nothing like it is to be seen anywhere in France. I am writing this at the school packed with coffins.… The centre wall in the gallery collapsed and buried the lithographs beneath – some were flung across the Gallery and shattered glass and broken frames is the worst that happened to them. The lithographs themselves happily and miraculously escaped injury.… At present the protection of the school, also badly shattered, from the weather and the care of our property and the other pictures is filling all my time.… Everybody is devoting their energies to relieving the terrible distress and finding homes for the 200,000 homeless and destitute.… Those pictures that were near the window sustained the damage from flying glass. I am packing these now.… There is hardly a whole pane of glass in our building and what glasses in the picture frames that *were* preserved, about 14, would be of great value to us if we might be allowed to keep them for we see no chance for many months to patch up our windows in the school

Figure 38
CONVOY IN BEDFORD
BASIN *n.d.*
oil on canvas
91.4 × 259 *cm*

and gallery.... I feel that you will understand our need in this.[3]

From the comparatively small amount of horror that Lismer had seen of the holocaust in Halifax, he could divine what was going on in the No Man's Land of trenches between France and Germany. His friend Jackson was painting *A Copse, Evening*, a scene of war wreckage that belied its peaceful name. His friend Varley wrote: "I tell you, Arthur, your wildest dreams pale before reality....and the only things worth thinking of are those intimate homely things, times when your kiddies have their nighties on and you sit by the fire with them before chasing them to bed and such like. I want to paint sunshine and burning golden leaves and blue waters, and laughing faces."[4] Instead, Varley was painting nightmare reality. He was at Ypres with its Sanctuary Wood and Hell Fire Corner pitted with shell holes "filled with dark, unholy water." He was painting khaki-clad dead being dumped into a cart mired in greasy grey-green mud. He called it *"For What?"* Varley established his reputation with his war pictures, but war was a horrible price to pay for a subject that would bring an artist fame.

The summer before the explosion was the time of Tom Thomson's tragic death. Lismer learned of it one afternoon when a Halifax friend remarked casually that he had just read in the paper that some artist in Ontario had been drowned. Then Frank Carmichael wrote him some details. On July 8th Thomson had taken his canoe to go fishing. His upturned canoe was found that day but his body was not discovered until the 17th. How did an expert woodsman come to such a mysterious end? No one knows for certain. Lismer was dazed. The Arts and Letters Club mounted a memorial exhibition in December. Lismer paid him tribute:

Thomson links...with the nature lover rather than the appreciator of aesthetic standards....Thomson sees visions and dreams. His paintings are his visions made articulate. He is not a primitive. He is an intuitive mystic. He felt nature, adored her, crept into her moods, and as paint was the only medium in which he was articulate, he painted, and his canvasses live in the Canadian mind and in the Canadian mold for those who needed such a revealer. He

Figure 39
91.4 × 259 *cm*
MURALS PAINTED BY
ARTHUR LISMER IN THE
GREEN LANTERN
RESTAURANT,
HALIFAX 1917
(*restaurant destroyed by fire*)

Figure 40
*Sketch from the artist's notebook
of Marjorie having her hair cut*

Figures 41–42
*Sketches from the artist's
Georgian Bay – Halifax
notebook*

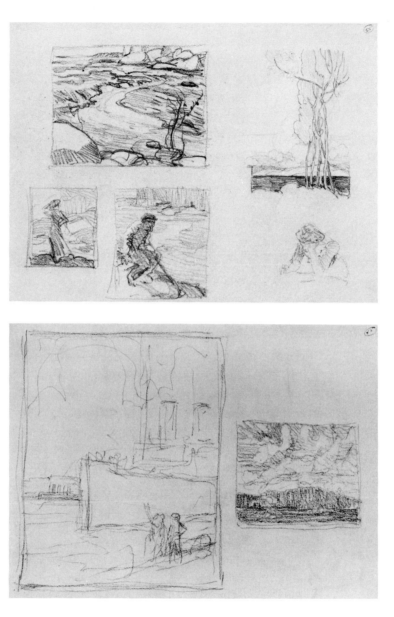

was themselves made articulate…He knew the stars, and the love
of woodcraft and the animals…like a sapling, or a deer in the forest.[5]

Life in Halifax was not all war or teaching. In addition to his
office in the school, Lismer rented a small studio for his
free-lance work. When W.L. Hart, owner of the Green Lantern Restaurant on Barrington Street, wanted to decorate the
banquet rooms with murals, he commissioned Henry Rosenberg to execute the mural for the ground-floor room and

Arthur Lismer to do the one for the second floor. One section of Lismer's mural was a happy scene of houses surrounding the Basin with hills in the background. Another depicted ships in the busy harbour and another patterned trees, art nouveau style. When the second and third floors of the restaurant were converted to offices during the Second World War, the murals were painted over. No one now knows in what order they were arranged, or the colours Lismer used to paint them for only black-and-white negatives remain.

Lismer also painted two other small murals during his Halifax years. One of light breaking from under sunset clouds over the sea was placed in a frieze-like arrangement over the doors of his office and the adjacent studio. The other was in the Lake Egmont country place of James E. Roy, a real estate man and

Figure 43
Arthur Lismer with Marjorie

Figure 44
Sketch of Esther Lismer reading

Figure 45
*Self-portrait from the artist's
sketchbook
charcoal on paper*

Figure 46
HALIFAX HARBOUR, TIME
OF WAR *c*.1917
oil on canvas
104.1 × 132.4 *cm*

director of the School of Art and Design.

The Nova Scotia countryside offered good painting country as well, and Lismer painted the river gliding by, and the loggers with their peaveys balancing on the logs that came down the Sackville River. He painted Esther out along the shore, or on their verandah high above the river. Esther would knit for hours as she waited for him to finish painting. He sketched her at home as she read. She complained that people would think that she never did anything but sit and read or sleep. He complained that she was still so seldom that he had to snatch at the few moments when she was quiet. He sketched his daughter often as she grew during these years.

He also sketched himself, not as a mercurial, quick-witted, fun-loving Arthur Lismer, but as a purposeful Lismer who had many ideals for the teaching of art, for the freedom but not licence of the artist, for the preservation of democratic government, for decent personal living. When Lismer's friend, Dr Barker Fairley of the Arts and Letters Club and one of the founders of the *Canadian Forum*, was shown the drawing in 1974, he remarked in his soft, still slightly Yorkshire-accented voice, "He rawther fawncied himself, didn't he?" It was an echo of the friendly joshing of the old Club days.

Some of Lismer's most notable works of these years were of war-time Halifax. One of his first paintings of the harbour, *Halifax Harbour, Time of War* (1916) included ships with smoke belching from their stacks under an enormous sky. In June of 1918 Eric Brown of the National Gallery gave Lismer a free hand to paint war subjects. Not officially commissioned as a war artist, he simply painted what he wanted and the Gallery took what it wanted. He had been in the eastern Canadian seaport long enough now to know the character and movements of the great ships, camouflaged with the dazzle system of curved or zigzaged lines, so that from a mile away it was difficult to see them on the sea. He went out on the minesweepers and the tugs, leaving early in the morning and returning at night.

In *Winter Camouflage* a great zigzagged liner lay on an ice-green sea with the blue of its marking repeated again in the far shore hills and the near shore snow. The pattern of colour on the hills, the pattern of the trees on the snow reflected

Plate 9
CONVOY AT SEA 1920
oil on canvas
163.2 × 213.3 cm

Plate 10
RAIN IN THE NORTH
COUNTRY *c.*1920
oil on panel
22.3 × 30 cm

Figure 47
ARRIVAL OF HOSPITAL
SHIP, PIER #2,
HALIFAX *n.d.*
lithograph
30 × 54 *cm*

Figure 48
THE SENTINELS *n.d.*
lithograph on wove paper
53.5 × 39.5 *cm*

nothing of any European school. *Convoy in Bedford Basin* depicted a panorama of six great ships, a tug and a tender on a long rectangular canvas. One camouflaged ship was placed just off centre and the expanse of water around it was broken by the wake of a tug and a tender. Another ship lay against the far shore, so effectively camouflaged that it melted almost invisibly into the shore even in the confines of the Basin. There was menace in these ships. They lay like a pod of sea serpents under the sky, ready to lash.

Lismer also made a series of superb finished drawings of war-time harbour scenes in charcoal or ink and lithographed some, including *Arrival of Hospital Ship Pier #2* and *The Sentinels*. These drawings are true, detailed and moving. One look at the angle of the bow of a tug rising upon a wave is enough to turn a land-lubber green.

At last the Armistice was signed, on November 11, 1918. The "war to end wars" was over and the boys were coming home. The rationing, the battle over conscription, the women who had worked long hours in the factories making bullets and bombs and who would now agitate for the vote, the wounded minus an arm or leg or both walking the streets of home, the mutilated beyond repair who would be hidden in the back rooms of hospitals, the war profiteers knighted for their patriotism – it was all over. Lismer was at the docks when the boys came home, and when Alex Jackson debarked, Lismer sketched him in uniform. They painted together again as in the

Figure 49
A.Y. JACKSON (*sketch from artist's notebook*) 1918
pencil on paper
25.4 × 19.9 cm

Figure 50
Marjorie and Esther Lismer on the day the AQUITANIA *returned, Halifax*

old days, for Jackson was still under commission for the War Records.

In 1919 Lismer mounted a one-man exhibition of eleven Halifax canvases and forty-two sketches, including *The Incoming Tide, Snow Pattern* and *Windy Weather*. They had been his relaxation from his endeavours to bring innovations into the conservative Victoria School of Art and Design, and from the repercussions of war. Not one sold. Nevertheless the advance in Lismer's technique was remarkable. From now on he would be a master of deep and varied colour and strong, sure patterning. He could transfer this artistic gain to landscape when the impetus arose. Could Halifax supply the impetus?

The penetrating, almost pugnacious look on the face revealed in the 1917 self-portrait was a determined Arthur Lismer, but where was he going now? He was thirty-four years old. Where was the dream of the national art movement that had sparkled in the conversation of his friends who were now returning to Toronto? What was he going to do about his wish to expand his interest in teaching art to children that his Saturday-morning art classes in Halifax had awakened in him? Much had happened during his three-year stay in Nova Scotia – Tom Thomson's death, the explosion, his little daughter reaching school age, his first picture sale to the National Gallery (*Road through the Bush*). Where did his future lie?

In April 1919, he received a letter from his friend Jim MacDonald, telling him to expect a letter from the principal of the Ontario College of Art offering him a post as vice-principal. A day later G.A. Reid's letter came with the offer. If Lismer accepted, it would mean leaving the good friends he had made in Bedford and Halifax, including Roy Zwicker, and architect Andrew Cobb and his wife Myrtle. Their daughter Elizabeth remembers Mrs Lismer as lovely, gentle, and not desirous of the limelight. Another was James E. Roy, one of the directors of the school. Sometimes, when Lismer dropped in for a visit, he liked to sit in the kitchen where Mrs Roy or her cook were making doughnuts. Lismer would eat them almost as fast as they could be fried. Lismer spoke of them all with affection.

Yet, it did not take him long to accept the offer of the Ontario College of Art; the school offered a far greater challenge than Halifax. His earnings would be almost double his

Figure 51
Arthur Lismer

present salary – $1,800 plus summer-school earnings. He would be back in the stimulating atmosphere of the Arts and Letters Club. Swiftly he recommended his successor in Halifax – Elizabeth Nutt, a "woman of spirit" from Sheffield – and prepared to return to Toronto. He was anxious to be back in the artistic thick of things. MacDonald's letter had said, "I haven't time to tell you about the old-fashioned row we had at the last meeting over the action of the hanging committee."[6] The thought of a little action again was irresistible. Who knew – there might even be an explosion in Toronto as great, if different in character, as the one he had witnessed in Halifax.

NOTES

1 Harold Beament to Lois Darroch, March 20, 1976
2 *Canadian Courier*, December 29, 1917
3 Arthur Lismer to Eric Brown, December 10, 1917, National Gallery of Canada
4 John A.B. McLeish. *September Gale: A Study of Arthur Lismer.* Toronto: J.M. Dent and Sons Ltd., 1955, p. 68
5 Unpublished manuscript in the possession of Marjorie Lismer Bridges
6 J.E.H. MacDonald to Arthur Lismer, April 23, 1919, National Gallery of Canada

Figure 52
Lake Superior

CHAPTER FIVE

The Infamous Coterie

The Halifax years had been productive ones for Lismer, and although he had chafed at some of the aspects of his life there, he had not just been marking time. He took the opportunity to develop his methods of teaching colour and design. He had learned that he liked teaching art to children and hoped that the way would open for broader efforts in Toronto. He had improved his painting technique to the point that he could make an effective picture out of lumbering battleships. He had produced a sufficient body of work of quality that he was elected an Associate of the Royal Canadian Academy.

The Royal Canadian Academy at that time was composed of a number of associate members: artists, designers and architects prominent in their respective fields who were entitled, when elected, to use the letters ARCA after their names. Full membership, or RCA, was restricted to about twenty-four in each category, and aspirants to the three-letter circle were obliged to wait until death cleared a place. Many ARCAS succumbed to the Grim Reaper themselves before they were elected full members. Although young artists have traditionally inveighed against the strictures of ruling academies, Lismer was delighted at the honour. And there was little likelihood of his putting a stranglehold on anyone's style.

Now that he was vice-principal of the largest art school in Canada, Lismer decided that he would buy a house. Until the Lismer family chose a location, they rented in Lawrence Park and in November 1919, they moved to 69 Bedford Park Avenue just a block from Yonge Street. There was no worry about paying for their substantial new possession. Sir Edmund Walker, chairman of the board of the National Gallery, had expressed his delight with Lismer's war paintings and drawings by purchasing a fair number of them for $2,250. It was half the price of the house.

At that time the house was on the outskirts of the city, and open fields stretched north of Lawrence Avenue. For a time Lismer shared an untidy studio with Alex Jackson while they completed their war-time paintings, but in 1921 he purchased the vacant lot to the east of his house and built a studio at the rear of it. The studio was an attractive place with a corner alcove panelled in wood salvaged from the old Normal School. A balcony loft on one side was useful for storing unsold canvases.

It was like the good old days as the artist friends lunched and dined once more in the effervescent atmosphere of the Arts and Letters Club, now in its new and grander quarters at 14 Elm Street. To Lismer the Club was "a kind of incubating ground ...we met a lot of people...like W.B. Yeats, people who were

important then....It was the one thing that tied me to Toronto."[1] The sadness was that Thomson was missing; no one was painting in Algonquin Park these days because of the memories he had left.

Harris, MacDonald, Johnston and Dr MacCallum were seeking new parts of Canada to paint. They had gone to the Algoma District twice, using Algoma Central boxcar No. ACR10557 as their headquarters and had returned as enthusiastic about that country as they had all been about Georgian Bay and Algonquin Park. Here everything was on an enormous scale. Mighty Lake Superior and miles and miles of mounded rocks stretched to the horizon. The landscape called them to portray the majesty and the starkness of this district just as they had done with others. In these surroundings MacDonald's style took a great leap forward. He painted *Solemn Land*, describing the country as "a panorama for the gods." Algoma would help to turn Harris toward spiritual abstraction and lead Lismer to his most ambitious paintings since the Halifax war canvases. In 1919 Harris, MacDonald and Jackson exhibited their Algoma works in their first independent exhibition.

The controversy over *The Tangled Garden* was still alive. To some viewers the work of the "bunch" still looked as if they had "scrambled their colours in a frying pan and laid them on with a paddle."[2] One night when they were spending an evening with Lawren Harris as host (Harris was a magnificent looking man; no one wore long hair then but his stood out around his head like an aureole with his bright eyes flashing beneath), the thought came to them of mounting another exhibition of nothing but their own works. Exhibitions were vitally important at a time when there were only three or four public art galleries in Canada and commercial art dealers were almost non-existent. Lismer and his friends were aggressive enough to mould a situation to suit themselves. They would not be immobilized when beleaguered by criticism of their new approach to Canadian painting. So on this evening in early 1920 the idea came to them of banding together in a kind of united front.

"How many are there here?" asked Lismer. "MacDonald, Harris, Johnston, Carmichael, Varley, myself, and Jackson who's in Penetang now will want to join. That makes seven. Why not call ourselves 'Group of Seven?'" So the Group of Seven they became, with Lismer, as he said, one of its "dumbfounders."[3] As the Group of Seven they would exhibit their pictures and bounce off their collective skin any further contumely that might assail their innovative approach to Canadian art.

The Group of Seven held their first exhibition in the spring of 1920 in the Art Gallery of Toronto. They made a simple statement of their aims:

> The group of seven artists whose pictures are here exhibited have for several years held a like vision concerning art in Canada. They are all imbued with the idea that an Art must grow and flower in a land before the country will be a real home for its people.... Recognizing that Art is an essential quality in human existence they will welcome and support any form of Art expression that sincerely interprets the spirit of a nation's growth.[4]

Lismer hung nine canvases – *The River Drivers, Logging, Halifax Harbour – Time of War, Spring in Nova Scotia, Springtime on the Farm, Winter, The Valley, Camouflage, The River* – and some sketches. Attendance was fair, about one hundred on a daily average, but only two canvases sold. Canadians still preferred European painting. MacDonald commented wryly: "We didn't sell enough canvases to make printing expenses. So it seems probable that we shall have to pay, as usual, for the privilege of giving the Toronto public an art education."[5] Public reaction was more tepid than expected, but there was the usual flurry of exchanges between the Artists' Table and the Knockers' Table in the Arts and Letters Club.

Nothing could dim the enthusiasm of the Group. They believed that to understand the country artists had to explore it rather than remain in their studios. In the spring of 1920 Lismer went to the Algoma District with Jackson, Harris, MacDonald and MacCallum. They were like boys exploring – up at six, out at eight for fresh sketches every day. One day when the rain was pouring down, Jackson recounted that Harris took his big sketching umbrella and went out as usual

Figure 57
A. Y. Jackson, Frank Johnston and Lawren Harris on the "Algoma Boxcar"

while Lismer remained in the tent. Nonetheless Lismer's busy instinct did not rest. As he lay with narrowed eyes gazing at his knapsack, the light sifting through the tent was pleasing and the folds of the knapsack took on a likeness to rock. When Harris came back dripping wet, Lismer was not only dry, he had a sketch in his box.[6]

Lismer returned from two trips to Algoma in the spring of 1920 and autumn of 1921 with the sketches that he would work into his magnificent *Isles of Spruce* and *Spring, Algoma.* He had been in his new country long enough to catch the great rhythm and balance of earth, sky and water, to describe the difference between his previous painting styles and what he wanted to do now. In his early attempts he had been "painting Canada to look a little bit like England, with soft hues and misty horizons. Canada is not like that and neither are its people. It is a country without shades and shadows, with bright colours and brutal changes of climate. Even the sun goes down with a bang .... Changes occur abruptly... the blazing colours embody a sense of the power of Canadian nature."[7]

He was beginning to see that "Morrice, Gagnon, Cullen, [Suzor-] Coté changed the Impressionist technique, giving it an even stranger excitement, but it does not transplant well in Canada. It is emotionally unstable, however scientific it may be, in our clear air and amid our solid form of land and water."[8]

Plate 11
ISLES OF SPRUCE 1922
oil on canvas
119.4 × 162.6 cm

Plate 12
A SEPTEMBER GALE,
GEORGIAN BAY 1921
oil on canvas
121.9 × 162.6 cm

Figure 60
GEORGIAN BAY 1926
brush and ink on paper
27.9 × 38.1 cm

Figure 61
EVENING SILHOUETTE 1928
oil on canvas
80.3 × 100.8 cm

With new insight Lismer had pitted his expertise against the solid land of the country, mile after purple, petrified, unyielding mile, or mile after mile of forest and swamp. Whether they knew it or not, Lismer and the Group of Seven had already passed from Impressionism to Post-Impressionism to their own distinctive style. The land and their determination had produced it.

In the autumn of 1920, between his two trips to Algoma, Lismer went again to Georgian Bay, the scene of his introduction to Canada's wonders. On this trip he was accompanied by Varley, newly released from the horrors of the last offensive of the war. Varley was free-lancing now, had just exhibited with the RCA and had been commissioned to paint a portrait of Vincent Massey. Lismer described him: "a man with a ruddy mop of hair and it *was* red – which burned like a smouldering torch on top of a head that seemed to have been hacked out with a blunt hatchet. That colour was the symbol of the fire in his soul."9

Lismer and Varley set out from the cottage one morning looking for a place to paint. On this particular day they both selected the same spot. Lismer won out and Varley took a vantage point a hundred feet away. The intensity of the scene soon engrossed them in the throes of creation. When they returned to Toronto, each enlarged his sketch into a canvas.

Lismer's became *A September Gale, Georgian Bay* and Varley's became *Stormy Weather*. Both were hung in the second exhibition of the Group of Seven. The Group again stated its credo:

> These pictures express Canadian experience and appeal to that experience in the onlooker. These are still pioneer days for the artists and after the fashion of the pioneers we believe whole-heartedly in the land. Some day we think that the land will return the compliment and believe in the artists, not as a nuisance or a luxury but as a real civilizing factor in the national life.[10]

Every member of the Group had reached full maturity now and Lismer was not the least among them. There is no need to analyze the mastery he displayed in reducing a turbulent, gusty scene into *A September Gale, Georgian Bay*. Some critics consider Varley's canvas superior to Lismer's and some *vice versa*. If interpretation of the elements of nature is the major criterion, Lismer's is superior. He had learned, among other things, to depict distance in his landscape, not merely with receding hues, but with all the contours and colours of a stormy day. In autumn the windy waters do not recede into calm as they do in Varley's picture. They are turbulent to the last inch of horizon. Lismer's painting caught this exactly. He also captured the power of the wind that marshalled the running waves. At the age of thirty-six he had reached a peak in his landscape-painting power.

On the whole, the second Group exhibition aroused as much praise as scorn, although there were some members who threatened to resign from the Art Gallery because it had hung such controversial pictures. Wrote one: "I must say that I have never seen such a conglomeration." Others affirmed, "They are not decadent but creative...their work is distinctive."[11] Augustus Bridle of the Toronto *Star* continued his support, and the young took eagerly to the brilliant paintings. Instead of examining them closely with microscopic expectation, they stood back and mixed the colours with their eyes as they were supposed to do. They were becoming modern landscape enthusiasts along with the men who painted.

The Group was now receiving notoriety outside the confines of Toronto and Montreal. It had been noticed in Ottawa in Parliament itself; the legislators of the land said that Lawren Harris was a menace, for they feared that his barren landscapes and realistic scenes of Toronto and Nova Scotia slums would discourage immigration. As director of the National Gallery, Eric Brown nearly lost his position twice for championing the new Canadian art, but he had the courage of his convictions. He had so little fear of the adverse effect of the Group that the Gallery already possessed about twenty-five of their major works and twenty-seven of Tom Thomson's.

The Group believed in their own work sufficiently to organize over forty smaller shows for Canadian towns and cities, and in 1922 they received the backing of the National Gallery for a year-long touring exhibition that caused a sensation across Canada. The greatest tribute of all came when a selection of the work of the Hot Mush School was sent in 1922 to the most important annual art show in the United States, the International Art Exhibition at the Pittsburgh Art Gallery, and in 1924 and 1925 to the British Empire Exhibition in Wembley, England.[12]

The jury to select the pictures for the Wembley show was appointed by the National Gallery, not by the Royal Canadian Academy which considered that it should have been the arbiter. Both the National Gallery and the Academy had been formed in 1880, and had pursued somewhat the same course until the advent of non-academic "rebel" artists such as the members of the Group. When Eric Brown insisted that the National Gallery choose the paintings for the Wembley Exhibition, the Academy was suitably upset at being excluded from the selection of the jury. Although Brown was clever enough to select artists who were also Academicians, the choice of the jury had been taken out of the Academy's hands. The controversy marked an irreparable break between the two institutions that would eventually result in their official separation by an Act of Parliament.

When critic Hector Charlesworth of *Saturday Night* learned who had made the Wembley choices (Lismer was on the jury), he wrote that the National Gallery was a "National Reproach." The exhibition actually represented a wide segment of Canadian art. Some three hundred paintings included works of Morrice, Gagnon and Walker, as well as those of the Group of Seven, including Lismer's *A September Gale*. When Charlesworth read London's appraisal ("These Canadian landscapes are the most vital group of paintings produced since the war, indeed in this century."), he erupted again: "Flub dub …what some of us has feared has come to pass. It was feared that the group of painters which elects to present in exaggerated terms the cruder and most sinister aspects of the Canadian wilds, would be accepted by the British critics as the most exclusive authentic interpreters of the Canadian landscape."[13]

But the pictures spoke for themselves. "Their bold decorative landscapes, emphasizing colour, line and pattern, give the very look and feel of Canada," claimed the London *Daily Chronicle*.[14] And another London paper wrote: "Canada, above all other countries, has reason to be proud of her contribution, her canvases are real triumphs…. Canada has arrived. She has a real national style…."[15] The infamous coterie, as Lismer dubbed the Group at times, had confounded those who had said there could be no Canadian art because Canada was an unpaintable country with no tradition or mythology from which to draw. They had wrested their own style from the land itself and had made their own tradition.

The Lismer family viewed this triumph of Canadian art first hand. His father had died the year before and so he took his family to see his mother and the Wembley show on his first trip home since his marriage.

The struggle to gain acceptance was now being rewarded. Each successive statement of the Group aims was more decisive than the last. In 1923 the introduction to the Group's catalogue was clear and bold:

New materials demand new methods, and new methods fling a challenge to the old conventions. It is as impossible to depict the pageantry of our northern woods with a lead pencil as it is to bind our young art with conventions and methods of other climates and other ages…. Artistic expression is a spirit, not a method, a pursuit, not a settled goal, an instinct, not a body of rules. In the midst of discovery and progress, of vast horizons and beckoning future, Art must take to the road and risk all for the glory of great adventure.[16]

Figure 62
PORTRAIT OF ERIC
BROWN *c.*1939
charcoal on wove paper
25.5 × 20.4 cm

It is a little startling after reading this jubilant statement to find Barker Fairley two years later writing about the Group: "By this time there must be fully two hundred people in Toronto who are genuinely interested in them. As art goes, this verges on a popular success."[17] Toronto's population then was about five hundred thousand.

The Group had triumphed but, like any art movement, its technique was now in danger of crystallizing into a somewhat basic composition of mounded rocks, water, and trees breaking the top edge of the canvas. The Group had painted, written, defended, inspired, innovated. God forbid that it should stagnate and let pines become as boring as cows in puddles.

This was unlikely, though by now each member had adopted some kind of favourite colour style. Jackson was turning to browns and ochres, Carmichael worked wonders with yellow, and MacDonald relished deep, rich tones. Harris used black and white for contrast, Varley could manage any subtle combination, and Johnston liked snow and its blue shadows. Lismer often employed green, the most difficult colour of all, and offset it with brilliant blue. But none of these men would degenerate into a set pattern of either colour or expression. By the middle of the twenties they were already visiting other localities and branching out to other forms in pursuit of their cause of painting Canadian.

In 1926 Harris made his first visit to the Canadian Rockies. The Algoma country had already moved him toward abstraction, and the majesty of the western mountains deepened this trend. Most Canadians were not ready for abstract art. "Mount Jello" or "Ice Cream Cone" mountains were the irreverent names given to two of his interpretations. In 1922 Frank Johnston decided that the adverse criticism of the Group was costing him sales when he needed money to support his family. He withdrew from his association with them and his noted winter scenes became a monetary mainstay. Frank Carmichael, still working for Rous and Mann in commercial art, had had his first painting purchased by the National Gallery in 1921. There was a faery quality to his work that made his landscapes distinctive. Foot-loose Jackson had extended his peregrinations as far west as the Skeena River with Edwin Holgate and Marius Barbeau, as far to the northwest as

Plate 13
GEORGIAN BAY *c.*1925
oil on panel
30 × 40.6 *cm*

Plate 14
QUEBEC VILLAGE 1926
oil on canvas
132.1 × 162.6 cm

Plate 15
THE MILL, QUEBEC 1925
oil on canvas
82 × 102.2 *cm*

Yellowknife, and up to the eastern Arctic as far as Pangnirtung, Baffin Island, with Frederick Banting of insulin fame. Varley had gone to teach at the Vancouver School of Art in 1926. MacDonald would paint in the Rockies for seven summers in a row.

In 1927 Lismer went to the Gaspé on a CNR pass that his friend Eric Brown had obtained for him. In 1928 he too went to the Rockies and painted *Cathedral Mountain*, now Mount Eisenhower. He wrote to Russell Harper:

We'd been painting in Georgian Bay and Algonquin Park where all the horizons were straight and the trees stuck up, and I suppose in the first days of the Group there was a sort of conventional pattern that crept into the work.... it was either spruce trees, or forest sticking above the horizon, but this Cathedral Mountain to me was like a great Gothic structure. It was an amazing thing. We were up about 6 to 7000 feet, I suppose, and from every angle and in a vast territory like this you had to talk to your prey, as it were, to find a way of getting at it.... there were buttresses and the pillars, towers and supporting weights like a vast piece of architecture and I think that in…the first way of looking at these things, we were looking for the design of the idea. I recall that most of the people in the Group of Seven, except MacDonald, never looked at their foregrounds. They looked right at the distance and I suppose this is the kind of adoration that you look up and find the glory – the clouds coming to it. You see as well the structure of the whole composition.... There was Temple Mountain, Castle Mountain, Cathedral. Always I think the original people who were responsible for naming these peaks had an idea that they were reminded of something in the edifices of the Church in history.

However, making the sketch was not difficult. It was comfortable enough in the clean air. And there's another thing – the atmosphere of the upper regions there. To approach it you passed through mountain Alpine meadows bestrewn with flowers and you were looking down on little lakes. You had a feeling of omniscience about the place and then you looked up to the top of these mountains. Well the idea was to reduce these forms away from the usual topographical photography that you see in brochures and so on and try to get some kind of design out of it.

Plate 16
CATHEDRAL
MOUNTAIN 1928
oil on canvas
121.9 × 142.2 cm

Figure 63
STUDY FOR CATHEDRAL
MOUNTAIN *c.*1928
black chalk with white highlights on green paper

And you begin to…see a rhythm that united sky and land…it was very challenging. When you got back to your studio it was a matter of composing it into, well, composing yourself and it into some kind of canvas that brought about those particular attributes. Another thing about that feeling, we were all ambitious for covering large surfaces…you can't reproduce a mountain on a small sketch and size…but the actual area of the canvas covered was a challenge. Cathedral Mountain is a memory. Looking down at a little green lake surrounded by the spruce and pine and looking up and seeing this thing soaring into the clouds which took up the rhythm and fetched it into an almighty paean of praise…. Mountains don't bend in the wind…they are cold and forbidding…[18]

Lismer's *Cathedral Mountain* is modern, almost cubist in its portrayal, but it is no ethereal, cold abstraction. It is mountain and mountain country all in one. It contains mountain height and majesty and beneath the haughty compelling grandeur are trees and an intimate jewel of a mountain lake. It is a vertical panorama.

There was no buyer for the painting in 1928. *Cathedral Mountain* was often exhibited but it remained unsold for a long time. "For years," said Lismer, "I had the largest collection of Lismers in Canada."[19]

No matter where Lismer traveled in the twenties there was always the Group to sustain him – that "despicable coterie," that "infamous quorum" as he liked to call it at different times. Many were the rousing conversations that took place in each other's homes or at the Arts and Letters Club, about Lismer's favourite poet, Walt Whitman, with his "barbaric yawp," or Plato, or Shaw, or Rabindrinath Tagore, the Indian poet who was popular then and whom Lismer would meet later as honourary president of the New Education Fellowship. There was a growing interest in Christian Socialism as an antidote to political unrest and one of its main exponents was Dr Salem Bland who wrote a column in the Toronto *Star* under the pseudonym of "The Observer."

Occasionally the lighter sessions of the artists and their friends would evoke some poetry. One poem by Sidney H. Hooke, a professor at the University of Toronto, was published in *The Rebel*. Hooke, a member of the Arts and Letters Club, was a professor of Oriental languages and literature who pinch-hitted in constitutional history during the First World War. He was a noted Hebraist and stated when he was called to the University that he could lecture in any of three or four departments. Hooke was so good in golf as well, that he made as much money as a pro giving lessons during the Depression as he was paid by the University. He also versified and once chose the Group of Seven as a subject.

THE BEATIFICATION OF THE BLESSED JAMES

St. Peter sat in drowsy state
At his golden desk at Heaven's gate,
And idly scanned each application
Of the candidates for beatification.
As his eye ran down the list of names
It fell on a certain MacDonald, James –
Profession – Artist,…
"Shiver my timbers! Why should I
O.K. another artist guy
Whose moniker's James? Just tell me that!
"Damned if I will," he said, "that's flat."
(*pause*)
Suddenly, crack! went the seven seals,
And boom! roared seven thunder peals,
And seven torches flared and guttered
As seven voices solemnly uttered
A dark and dreadful imprecation
At the man who refused beatification
Of any one of the School of Seven.
From the awful silence then in Heaven –
"You'll be damned if you don't," said Lawren Harris,
"You'll be damned if you don't,"said Arthur Lismer
And Professor Robins replied, "Amen"…
This is the way the beatification
Of James took place by acclamation;
And if you don't believe my simple tale
See Lismer's picture of the halo.[20]

Dr John Robins, who replied, Amen, likely with the usual twinkle in his brown eyes, was a professor of English at

Victoria College. He was noted for his huge laugh, his knowledge of Old English, his interest in his students as individuals,
his deep-voiced telling of Uncle Remus and Paul Bunyan
stories, and his jovial, engaging contemplation of Algonquin
Park in *The Incompleat Angler*. He was also a member of the
Arts and Letters Club. Association with other creative minds
in the Club was a constant inspiration to the members of the
Group.

The Group and the Arts and Letters Club supplied a satisfying social life for Lismer, but there was also entertaining to
be done in Toronto in the Lismers' new home. Their personal
entertaining was usually confined to two or three people for
dinner or the evening. In the summer there would be "garden
suppers" at the studio, and in the winter there would be
Sunday high teas, the fashion of the time, with a group of
friends.

Elizabeth Nutt, who was holding tight rein at the Victoria
School of Art and Design in Halifax, stayed with the Lismers
for two summers when she was teaching the summer courses in
art. She was a wonderful character and a redoubtable talker,
intensely interested in everything. The only escape for the head
of the household those summers was to go into the garden in
which Miss Nutt did not like to work. The Lismer garden was
very well tended during those two summers. Lismer enjoyed
teasing her for she rarely failed to rise to his bait and never
learned to distinguish between the times when he was serious
and when he was pulling her leg.

What the seven artists would have achieved had they not
reinforced each other by their accidental agglomeration is anyone's guess. When an interviewer in the early sixties asked
Lismer what the other members of the Group meant to him, he
answered:

> These individuals were not the rebels they were supposed to be.
> They were people excited about their own country, and I think a
> lot of the infection we got from one another…was by mutual
> observation, actually travelling over the country…. Aesthetically
> it was virgin territory. I, as an Englishman coming from the north
> of England…had been soaked in traditional English land. Here
> was something new and it was the newness of it that created the
> infamous coterie known as the Group of Seven. Everything about

it was something that fired the imagination.[21]

Again and again Lismer was asked to explain the workings of the Group. In 1942 as he eulogized his friend Jackson, he described them as "That strange little coterie of embattled painters looking for fun and finding trouble. They took life seriously, art lightly and their Canadianism seriously, but were blithely unconscious of anything in the way of making history."[22]

By the end of the twenties the Group of Seven had accomplished its purpose of painting the Canadian scene in a Canadian way. Its own success had created a school of followers that was in as much danger of placing a stranglehold on Canadian art as the proponents of early Dutch landscape painting. As Lismer was fond of quoting, "Imitation is not the sincerest form of flattery. It is an insult."[23] The oncoming Depression and its attendant hardships made a school of landscape painters seem a little out of touch with reality, and most people tended to forget that art provided a moment's respite from a situation that tried men's souls. The alluring concept of the artist as romantic adventurer in the wilds had had its hour. So, to some extent, had the concept of nature as a challenge to the imagination, a dream embodied in such popular literature of the decade as the books of Charles G.D. Roberts and Ernest Thompson Seton.

The members of the Group were already scattered. Now the time had come for them to disband. Johnston's place had been filled by Alfred J. Casson, a colleague of Frank Carmichael's at Rous and Mann. Varley was still in Vancouver heading the department of drawing and painting at the School of Art. Jim MacDonald, never a robust man, was working beyond his strength as principal of the Ontario College of Art. Harris and Jackson were as usual independent in their comings and goings. Edwin Holgate and Lemoine Fitzgerald were asked to join in 1931, but in that same year the Group of Seven held its final exhibition. On December 5, 1931, at a reception in Lawren Harris's spacious house on Ava Road, A.Y. Jackson made the announcement that the Group was disbanding.

In 1932, the year Jim MacDonald died, the Group of Seven melded into the thirty-member Canadian Group of Painters. It would never have the camaraderie of the smaller Group. Its membership fluctuated from year to year, with some artists exhibiting only once. Other painters were complaining that the "Seven Wise Men" had become so successful that they were dominating Canadian art from Toronto, so the membership was drawn from across Canada. Its first exhibition was held in Atlantic City, New Jersey, in 1933, and was characterized as an "outgrowth of the Group of Seven," representing the modern movement in Canadian painting.

The Canadian Group of Painters included women such as the West Coast's Emily Carr and Toronto's Doris Heustis (Mills Speirs), Paraskeva Clark, Yvonne McKague (Housser), Isabel McLaughlin and Kathleen Daly (Pepper). The latter three had studied abroad and later became involved in the Art Students' League, a student breakaway from the Ontario College of Art that was intended to encourage freedom of spirit. Other members of the Canadian Group of Painters included Carl Schaefer, Charles Comfort who had decided to become a painter when he viewed the first Group of Seven exhibition, and Bertram Brooker who had held the first exhibition of abstract painting in Canada at the Arts and Letters Club in 1927.

During the decade of the great days of the Group, Canada had become more knowledgeable in art. In April 1927, two months after Brooker's show, Lawren Harris's personal influence brought to the Art Gallery of Toronto the collection of the Société Anonyme. It included works by Mondrian, Duchamp, Kandinsky, Stella and other ultra modernists. Be it said to Toronto's credit that no one fainted during the exhibition – but neither did many of the Canadian viewers turn easily to abstraction.

Groups may come and go – Automatistes, Painters Eleven, Regina Five, lyric abstractionists – and invariably some of the new ones will be thought as outrageous as the "infamous coterie." But there never has been an art movement in Canada like the Group of Seven. They transcended their influences and in doing so they produced a body of landscape art unparalleled in the history of Canada.

No group has endeared itself, even enshrined itself, in the hearts of Canadians as has the Group of Seven. To them has been accorded, and it can be said without bathos, something akin to love. They are one of Canada's national treasures and rightly will remain so.

NOTES

1 Undelivered interview for CBC radio, c.1964
2 Peter Mellen. *The Group of Seven.* Toronto: McClelland and Stewart Limited, 1970, p. 64
3 Harry Hunkin. *There is no Finality...A Story of the Group of Seven.* Toronto: Burns and MacEachern, 1971, p. 86
4 *Ibid.* p. 91
5 *Ibid.* p. 91
6 A.Y. Jackson. *A Painter's Country.* Toronto: Clarke, Irwin & Company Limited, 1958, p. 47
7 Undelivered interview for CBC radio, c.1964
8 Arthur Lismer. "A.Y. Jackson, LL.D., Painter of Canada: An Appreciation," January 30, 1942, (speech in manuscript), Art Gallery of Toronto
9 Arthur Lismer. *F.H. Varley Paintings 1915–1954: The Early Years.* Toronto: Art Gallery of Toronto, 1954
10 H. Hunkin. *There is no Finality...A Story of the Group of Seven.* p. 99
11 P. Mellen. *The Group of Seven.* p. 101
12 Lismer pictures exhibited: *A September Gale – Georgian Bay, Logging, Nova Scotia, Rocks, Pine and Sunlight*, six lithographs from the war, *Isles of Spruce, The Happy Isles, McGregor Bay, Georgian Bay* (pencil drawing), *Pine*
13 Ken Johnstone. "The Professor is a Rebel," *New Liberty*, May 1951, pp. 32–33, 44–52
14 Graham McInnes. *A Short History of Canadian Art.* Toronto: Macmillan Company, 1939, p. 83
15 H. Hunkin. pp. 115, 116
16 F.B. Housser. *A Canadian Art Movement.* Toronto: Macmillan Company, 1926, p. 157
17 Barker Fairley. "The Group of Seven," *Canadian Forum*, v, no. 53 (February 1925), p. 144
18 Arthur Lismer to Russell Harper, no date
19 John A.B. McLeish. *September Gale: A Study of Arthur Lismer.* Toronto: J.M. Dent and Sons Ltd., 1955, p. 51
20 Lismer file, Metropolitan Toronto Library, no date
21 Undelivered interview for CBC radio, no date
22 Arthur Lismer. "A.Y. Jackson, LL.D., Painter of Canada: An Appreciation"
23 *The New Outlook.* August 22, 1934

Figure 64
The Ontario College of Art,
Toronto 1924

CHAPTER SIX

Child Art, Toronto

During his creative years with the Group of Seven, Arthur Lismer was employed full time, first as vice-principal of the Ontario College of Art and principal of the summer school teachers' course, and then as educational supervisor of the Art Gallery of Toronto. It was not exactly the program of a dilettante, and Lismer breezed into the work of his new position with all the pent-up enthusiasm he had been building during the three years in Halifax. In an early article in the *Canadian Courier*, "Art and the Average Canadian," he indicated his feelings: "I do not believe there is a university in the country with a chair in Fine Arts."[1] The College of Art was not a university, but he intended nevertheless to proselytize in the field of art education, as well as painting.

Lismer did manage to find time to paint as he coped with the innumerable details of a position that was part teaching and part administrative. Did he regret not being able to paint full-time? One thing was certain – he had accepted the position and whatever he committed himself to do, he would do well. From now on he would become a summer painter, for that was the only time he could get away to sketch. The dichotomy did not bother him; teaching was as much a cause with him as landscape painting. There was no topside to the coin of Arthur Lismer's twin talents. He wrote: "As a painter, I'm a good educator. As an educator, I'm a good painter."[2] And again, "having to make a decision between the life of a painter and that of a teacher, I managed to do both."[3] Professional artists, he said, were often poor teachers, and he prided himself on his own double ability.

He was now vice-principal of the largest art school in Canada. It had had humble beginnings in 1876 when the Ontario Society of Artists opened the Ontario School of Art in one long room at 14 King Street West, with the assistance of a one-thousand-dollar grant from the province. In 1890, with the new name of the Ontario School of Art and Design, it moved to three rooms in the Normal School, on the site of the present Ryerson Polytechnical Institute. In 1920 the school was preparing to move to McCaul Street adjacent to the Art Gallery, where it assumed the name of the Ontario College of Art. What could be more propitious for the work Lismer had in mind?

When Lismer assumed his duties the principal was George A. Reid, president of the Royal Canadian Academy from 1906 to 1909, and principal of the College since 1912. After the promise of his early *Mortgaging the Homestead* and *Forbidden Fruit*, Reid's later canvases had become somewhat stereotyped and uninteresting. When his classes at the College assembled

Figure 65
SUNLIGHT IN A WOOD
(*sketch*) 1929
crayon on paper
27.9 × 37.8 *cm*

Plate 17
SUNLIGHT IN A WOOD 1930
oil on canvas
91.4 × 101.6 *cm*

every autumn, he assigned them a spot for their easels, saying, "Now that's yours till spring and don't move from it even if you don't like your view of the model."

Lismer's temperament was different, and his inexhaustible energy penetrated every aspect of the school, its curriculum and its students. He would burst into the room waving his arms and say, "Students, I'm glad to see you here. You all want to be artists? Well, it'll take some doing. Let's get at it."

Lismer felt that discipline at the College was lax since pupils with little dedication to their work were allowed to remain in the school. Many procedures were in strong contrast to the decorum that had prevailed at the Sheffield School of Art when Lismer himself was a student, but reprimand or suspension would have cost the school a fee-paying student in times when juggling College finances was difficult enough.

In spite of the frustration that Lismer felt early in his teaching time in Toronto, he had no intention of giving up. In March 1920, Eric Brown wrote that the director of the Carnegie Institute in Pittsburgh was thinking of hiring an assistant from outside the United States. In spite of the prestige the move would have entailed, Lismer was not interested, for it meant:

...leaving Canada and getting away from the centre of develop-

Plate 18
BAIE ST PAUL, QUEBEC 1931
oil on canvas
66 × 81.2 cm

Plate 19
GLACIER ABOVE MORAINE
LAKE 1926
oil on canvas
101.5 × 126.7 cm

Plate 20
SOMBRE ISLE OF PIC, LAKE
SUPERIOR *c.*1927
oil on canvas
86.4 × 110.5 cm

ment of art in this country and I've had my experience of that sort
of thing in Halifax.... I find it pretty hard to continue painting
and teaching – they don't go together very well. The art school
has a big enrolment and we are fearfully limited for room and
have a very useless system and little discipline. The task of applying a thorough form of art instruction becomes tiresome at
times. I've still more respect for G.A. Reid and what he has tried
to do for the art school here – but he is too amiable and gentle,
and badly supported by a staff who have no idea of working
together. We are having a new building on the "Grange" property going up this year, but as far as I can see there is no thought of
any new spirit going into it.[4]

In his own classes of drawing, composition and design, his
first concern was to set high standards and demand the best. He
wanted students to stretch themselves even if they failed, for
the next time they might succeed. His attitude in general was
kindly, but he became impatient if it was obvious that a student
was ill prepared. He rarely drew over a student's work as some
instructors did, but would demonstrate on a separate sheet
how to make a line light or dark. One time he came up behind a
young man who was caricaturing his teacher secretly, or so he
thought. "Here," said Lismer to the startled student, "you'll
never get me that way. This is how."

Once a scholarship student, Helen Sanderson (Sewell),
looked over at the work of another top scholar with whom she
was competing for first place. He was doing such good work
that she fell into the temptation of imitating it. When Lismer
came along, he just said quietly, "You have your own style.
Stick with it."

In design classes he wanted the students to think out their
assignments for themseves. If the design was to be for a teapot,
it had to be relevant to the material specified – if ceramic, one
piece; if pewter or copper, strengthened where the seams
joined. They had to learn the difference between designing for
textiles with a weave, or linoleum made from liquid that hard-
ened after pouring. The students had to be tough enough to
take hard work.

In 1926, when a wing that comprised two galleries, a sculpture court and a print room was added to the main Art Gallery

Figure 66
The class at the Ontario College of Art, Toronto c. 1928 (including Roy Mitchell, A.Y. Jackson, Yvonne McKague Housser, J.W. Beatty, Emanuel Hahn, Arthur Lismer)

building, Lismer put the new facilities to immediate use. One day he was helping a group appreciate Renaissance art by building a verbal picture of the life of the time – the high-coiffured, full-skirted ladies, the palaces, the fountains. "You can almost hear those fountains." He paused, and the silence was filled with the gentle sound of the falling of the water in the fountain the middle of the Gallery court. "You might almost hear the music of the lutes." A phonograph filled the court with soft music. "You might imagine that one of the court ladies was about to come in and sit down in that chair so that you could paint her as the artists of those days used to do."[5] A tall girl dressed in the costume of the period walked quietly in and sat down in the chair. Without a word, the class went to work.

Inevitably, there were some who found his standards stultifying. Once the students entering the sculpture room found that Lismer had thrown his coat over a sculpture that displeased him. He pinned a note on his coat that said, "Please remove." It was a depiction of a couple in close embrace, taboo for the time. Fourth-year students were allowed nude models, but paintings of nudes were frowned on in most circles. It had only been twenty-five years since Thomas Eakins had been forced to resign from his position with the Pennsylvania Academy of Fine Arts for allowing a completely nude male

Figure 67
LISMER WITH LADIES IN
ART CLASS *n.d.*
charcoal on paper
12.7 × 19.3 *cm*

Figure 68
*Class in progress at the Ontario
College of Art, Toronto*

model to sit for the women's life class. Paul Peel had painted his little models with only their sweet backsides presented to the viewer, and Holgate had not yet begun to recline his monumental nudes on rocks. Lismer had drawn nude models in both Sheffield and Antwerp, but in some ways he was still a man of his time.

He entertained as he talked and his lectures often shone. He was never the same twice. When the occasion demanded he could be formal and precise; he could be slapdash at others. When overcome with enthusiasm, or with boredom at going over the same ground so often, he would fidget, scratch his back, and violate all the canons of good delivery. Most of the students loved him too much to complain.

The College of Art in the twenties was like one large family, with Lismer a surrogate father. The students worked hard, but they had fun, too, and their teacher often shared it with them. At noon he might join them in Grange Park when spring enticed them outdoors, his hair flying away from his balding pate. Or he would playfully take a hand in a baseball game. Once at least, toward the end of a student party, he helped a girl out a back window as her father came storming in at the front door so that she could arrive home before being found out.

Figure 69
*Arthur Lismer and Madge
Gough at the Beaux Arts Ball,
the Ontario College of Art,
Toronto*

The social highlight of the year at the Ontario College of Art was the Beaux Arts Ball for which the students researched and designed their own costumes. In 1923, the year of the discovery of the boy King Tutankhamen's tomb, the theme was Egyptian. On the walls was a stylized frieze of Egyptian court officials bearing the features of staff members such as Arthur Lismer, Jim MacDonald, Emanuel Hahn and George Reid.

The role of vice-principal of any school is not necessarily a satisfying one. It depends on whether the principal will delegate some of the creative work or just saddle him with routine matters. When Lismer accepted the post of vice-principal and assumed his duties of teaching drawing and composition, he had expected that the new approaches to colour and pattern that he and the Group were adopting would be allowed. Reid, however, favoured older methods. But Lismer was not cut out to be a cipher no matter what his position. He also wanted to expand the work of the College to include extension classes for students of varying ages, from pre-schoolers to adults. He believed the College should be a force in the community, instead of teaching only those of high-school age. He wanted to reform the courses of instruction and was becoming increasingly discontented with Reid's easygoing and traditional approach. The lack of supervision was resulting in slackness among the students and poor cohesion among the staff which was, like that of any art college, formed of creative individuals intent on their own production as well as their teaching, and not necessarily ready to act in concert. The composition of the staff fluctuated from year to year as well, making continuity difficult.

The students felt the friction and some of them left, despairing of a change for the better. They formed the independent Art Students' League, housed at 4 Grange Road and supervised by Edna Breithaupt, Alex Jackson's second cousin, as a kind of house mother.

In 1927, with no hope for change at the Ontario College of Art, Lismer resigned as vice-principal and began work at the Gallery. "This country," he wrote a little later to Harry McCurry, Eric Brown's assistant at the National Gallery, "is fifty years behind in Art Education, and Ontario is the most backward province in the Dominion."[6] He intended to use every ounce of his energy to change the face of art education. An education committee of five people was formed at the Gallery, and one of its members was Arthur Lismer. When the committee recommended that "a competent person be appointed to supervise and complete arrangements initiated by the Education Committee,"[7] no one answered the description better than the man who may even have helped word the proposal. He would promote tours and lectures, he would train instructors and docents, he would change the Gallery from a building genteel people visited on a Sunday afternoon into a place of teeming activity. He had seen "the foolish panoply" of war,[8] and felt that if he could bring beauty into people's lives, they might forget petty differences. The place to change the social order was in the minds of children, and this could be effected through a change in the teaching of art.

At that time most public schools taught art in half a Friday afternoon per week, with little equipment and not much imagination. At Hallowe'en, the children traced pumpkins and witches; at Christmas, Santa Claus and snowflakes; at Valentine's, hearts; at Easter, yellow chicks. In between, they were given chalk boxes to draw as a means of learning perspective or they tried to copy pictures of rainbows and puppies from "art books" supplied by the Department of Education. That a child should draw or paint what he wanted in a way native to him was outside pedagogical practice.

In September 1927 Lismer began his work from a little office set up in a corner of the Grange print room. Now at last he could work toward his objective. He had had time in Halifax to "study the growth and personality of a child: this has nothing to do with talent. Art is the only way a three-year-old can communicate; he can't talk much, he can't read, and doesn't reveal much – except through his drawings." He had seen too much of "the sad little array of colour studies, the timid fine-lined drawings of sick-looking flowers, the ellipses and vanishing lines, the spouts and handles." That was no way to teach children. "No child likes to be asked to draw a jam jar....If the children are told to do what they like, they will reveal what they are."[9] Once again Lismer was an innovator – this time in the teaching of child art.

The first thing to do toward changing current teaching attitudes was to show what could be done. An exhibition of children's art from the classes of a Viennese teacher, Franz Cizek, was then touring the United States and Europe. Lismer arranged for it to come to Toronto.

When Cizek was a student at the Academy of Fine Arts in Vienna, he boarded with a carpenter who had a number of children. When the children borrowed his painting materials, they produced such adventurous work that Cizek realized that they had an inner world of their own that they needed to express in their own way. In the art schools of their day they were being taught to copy designs from the board with little pencils and little brushes that were unsuited to their limited motor ability. As soon as he could, Cizek formed his own juvenile art class. There he allowed the children to express their creativity in a mode suitable to them. His creed was: "There is an art that children create for themselves. The child makes pictures and drawings, not for grown-ups, but to make real his own desires, inclinations, and dreams." Teachers had to work fast to give a child a chance. "There is much of autumn and winter in life, but spring never comes again,"[10] wrote Cizek.

Arthur Lismer had never met Franz Cizek or seen the work he was doing, but he had heard all about it. In May 1927, Cizek's exhibition of child art arrived at the Art Gallery of Toronto. Lismer gave it wide publicity and about twelve hundred children viewed it. The general public was astonished at the colour, design and imagination displayed. It was "a magnificent demonstration of what children could do under *guidance*, not strict control." This was what he too intended to do with children.

By using Cizek's informal approach, Lismer hoped to revolutionize the teaching of art. His first aim was "to train our teachers to treat the child as a developing human being…to remember that you start with a child and you help the child be a child whilst he is one."[11] The second was to hook the child early on art, and encourage an appreciation of aesthetics. This would eventually create for artists the kind of knowledgeable public they deserved.

For two years Lismer worked with the education committee, organizing tours and lectures under Gallery auspices. He inaugurated special Gallery visits for children. There had been a time when children were not allowed into libraries. He was determined that the Gallery would never be out of bounds to them. Children were still not allowed to speak above a whisper in the unnatural hush of libraries. That too would not prevail in the Gallery. He held special lectures for teachers who in turn would encourage children to come.

He organized Saturday morning classes for the eight- to fourteen-year-old children of Gallery members. It was a beginning, but being the child of a member did not necessarily mean that the child wanted to draw. It was too small a section of the public to depend on and the classes were not successful. He soon realized that the source to tap was the city as a whole. Knowing that schools were the key to continuing numbers, he began to lobby members of the Board of Education.

His enthusiasm was catching, and his early attempts were bearing fruit. In April 1929, he brought a second Cizek exhibition that inspired as much enthusiasm and wonder as the first. In October he was appointed supervisor of education at the Gallery at double his former salary. The time was now ripe to begin a full program of child art.

He announced that Saturday morning art classes would begin at the Gallery in February 1930. What an optimist he was to begin in frozen February! On February 8th, several hundred children recommended by their teachers came from all over Toronto to take a test for admission to the classes. They were asked to select a work of art from anywhere in the Gallery and do what they could with it on paper. The lucky ones would be accepted for the free classes and free materials.

The following week the three hundred chosen students appeared on the steps of the Gallery. They formed a cross-section of Toronto's social and ethnic population. Five instructors were selected from the recent graduates of the Ontario College of Art – students such as Erma Lennox (Sutcliffe) and Tillie Cowan. Dorothy Medhurst (Hoffman) came from Central Technical School. Lismer himself was always present to provide a stimulating introduction to the morning's work.

These classes did not teach copying. They encouraged creativity and individuality. The children were provided with huge sheets of paper, big brushes, and paints or crayons. They worked as they wished. No one told them what colour to paint an elephant or where to put the berries. They wiggled and twisted and sprawled everywhere they could find space, mostly on the floor on cushions. The classes looked like chaos to orthodoxy, and there were great protests when principals or Board of Education members came to observe. A.Y. Jackson came, looked, and departed. He had no hand with children, but he had faith in his friend. Gradually, the objectors realized that this strange phenomenon had come to stay. Before long there were five hundred children in the Saturday morning classes.

Lismer was a natural with the children. He cultivated a few simple tricks to capture their attention. He could balance a lump of sugar on his elbow and with a swift move catch it in his hand. He was loosely jointed. "Break my wrist, break my elbow, break my arm," he would say, as he performed strange gyrations with his joints. As a child, he had been left-handed, but was encouraged to write with his right. After his right arm was badly broken, he was allowed to be left-handed again. He became ambidextrous and could write backwards with one hand and forwards with the other simultaneously. He could imitate the sound of a flute or birds. All these little tricks helped relieve tension in a new group. He would come into a strange class armed only with a list of names, or sometimes without any names. "Let's see now, which one is Anne?" A hand would shoot up and the little faces would light up as they waited to be recognized by this engaging Merlin.

He never seemed to be at a loss for a way to hold children's attention. After he had established a mood, he would sketch swiftly as they watched – not enough to discourage, just enough to inspire. He did inspire, and just as important, he took the children seriously at a time when they were taught that children should be seen and not heard. Here was a man who encouraged them to express themselves. At school they were told they must copy. Here was a man who was actually excited when they did what they wanted to do, who could look at things from their point of view, who never ran out of ideas and projects.

Figure 70
SAMMY SUMAC *n.d.*
Pencil and oil pastel on paper
16.5 × 16.5 cm

Figure 71
*Saturday morning class in
progress at the Art Gallery of
Toronto* 1936

Lismer was keen on organizing group projects that taught children to work together, although group projects were considered a revolutionary teaching method in the early thirties. These projects usually took the form of pageants for which the participants improvised their own costumes and painted their own scenery after a study of the subject. As they were waiting for the performance of a Biblical pageant, one little boy worked up a headache from the excitement and was sent off to find an aspirin. "We'll have to wait a moment for Moses," said Lismer, "he's gone to get a tablet." The punster in him never slumbered.

When Saturday morning was over and the children had trooped home, the instructors would gather with Lismer for an afternoon criticism session. "Why did you do a five-year-old thing with the eight-year-olds?" he might fire at one teacher. She would fire back at him defending her choice, or she would acknowledge that her procedure had been ill chosen and accept advice. Everyone was treated equally and everyone helped everyone else, just as the Group of Seven had done in another sphere. Lismer was a genius at guiding without laying down the law, both with teachers and children.

Many of Lismer's "babies" went on right to the top, including Aba Bayefsky, Paul Duval, John Hall and William Withrow, director of the Art Gallery of Ontario since 1961. Countless others have carried the influence of the Saturday morning classes with them in other careers.

In addition to children, Lismer taught teachers in summer courses, extension classes at the University of Toronto, night classes at Central Technical School (at that time the only school in Toronto that taught more than one year of art in the first year of high school), and an eager group at newly opened Hart House. In time his former students were teaching outside Toronto – Dorothy Medhurst in Aurora, Audrey Taylor in Oshawa, Gordon Payne in Ingersoll. Lismer's teachers found him an exacting master, but were absolutely devoted to him. Beneath the facade of the witty man who joked and played, there worked a highly critical intelligence that encouraged them to give their best.

All this work was seminal, but again Lismer was the butt of criticism, this time not for his painting but for his teaching methods. He shrugged it off more easily now, for he was too well established to let it bother him. Some of the teachers who tried to follow his methods interpreted freedom of expression to mean total lack of direction. They failed because they let their pupils linger too long in the free-expression period. Sooner or later students had to learn about perspective and styles, but if these were taught at the proper time, there would be less discouragement.

Lismer's work was prospering. He was making an art of teaching art. The numbers in the Saturday morning classes never lessened, and attendance was being constantly maintained by another of Lismer's innovations – tours of the Gallery under the sponsorship of the Toronto Board of Education. School tours became part of the regular curriculum and soon sixty schools were participating.

In October 1933, another of Lismer's dreams came true when a Children's Art Centre was opened at 4 Grange Road, in the house that had been vacated by the disbanding Art Students' League. This was Lismer's own experimental child art centre, the first in the British Commonwealth. The Centre became a reality through a grant from the Carnegie Corporation. The total budget for 1935 was $16,000, with $10,000 coming from the Corporation. The teachers were paid a dollar an hour, and pupils were chosen from the best eleven- to thirteen-year-olds in the Saturday morning classes. They attended after school three afternoons and one evening a week.

In 1935, the work of Toronto's children was shown in an international exhibition of child art in New York and a later exhibition in England. Four years later, a spring exhibition of child art in Toronto was reviewed enthusiastically by the same Augustus Bridle, Toronto *Star* critic, who over twenty years before had attended the first exhibition of the Group of Seven. "Forget all preconceived notions of the merely conventional in art as you look over this scenario of vast everyday illusions," he wrote. In ten years at the Saturday classes and the Children's Art Centre, Lismer had given 12,000 children the opportunity to "let their souls come forward."

Lismer knew the value of publicity. He gave his first radio broadcast in the early 1930s, and in 1936 he wrote a book entitled *Education Through Art for Children and Adults at the*

Art Gallery of Toronto, an account of his work during the previous six years. He also published an article in the *Canadian Forum*:

> Growth is the fundamental process of all life, and following as it does a divine order of progression and beauty, it holds the core and clue to the character and quality that education for the young should follow. The creative character of childhood is a powerful yet tender plant – feed it on patent food, regiment it, support it with crutches and the hardy bloom that it should have been becomes a forced and sickly plant, non-creative of further growth. We are so far ahead of our primitive culture that we have lost sight of their forms and designs. Our refined instincts are so hostile and so overlaid by the accumulations of society that we cannot grasp the surging life and creative necessity that primitive origins of our society once possessed. But children are primitives, indeed they are the prototypes of ancient man, or pre-historic man, or whatever stage in the development of mankind wherein the things they do are not separated from the ordinary functions of existence.

> One reason for the lack of creative elements in the school programme is that most adults regard art as a wasted period in public instruction...a frill or fad that has no place in the stern business of life. Consequently, the sight of five or six hundred children drawing and painting in an art gallery for no other reason to the children but that they enjoy doing it, is a unique and disturbing sight to grown people.[12]

And in the *Dalhousie Review* he wrote: "The modern idea of Art in education accepts the vital truth that true education should aim at the harmonious development of native abilities, instead of using the child as an example of obedient response to professional or commercial demands."[13]

So Lismer continued to fly in the face of traditional art teaching. His Group of Seven friends realized the importance of what he was doing. A.Y. Jackson wrote that Lismer's insight had "influenced the entire art education of our country."[14] Now this influence was spreading across the country. Classes based on his principles were being established in Oshawa,

Cornwall, Sarnia, Halifax and the Maritimes, Montreal, Winnipeg, Edmonton and Vancouver. One of Toronto's staff members, Freda Pepper, set up a program in Detroit. In future years, Lismer himself would travel to South Africa, Australia and New Zealand on similar missions.

In the thirties, as the world slid on its way to war, Lismer's emphasis on free expression and the things of the spirit had a deeper implication than it might have had in any other decade. He wrote in 1936:

> The claims of art as a guiding star in education are as valid and important as the moral, physical, scientific and economic aspects in the development of a new society. People without art are fit for 'stratagems and spoils,' and go goose-stepping to every blare of dictator music, joining with the mob of other servile ones in the spurious march to a possessive theme of fear and hatred...a man-made chaos of war, intrigues and mob hysteria.[15]

A decade earlier he had noted that "The art of a nation is the expression of the nation's presence on the path that leads towards things of the spirit.... It is the expression of a nation's will to create, not its will to power."[16]

Those with only a will to power were now in the ascendancy and those with a will to prevent them were often labeled subversives. Some of his children's art teachers were involved in the Canadian Youth Congress, an organization that was aware that changes must come in the economic order if a second world war were to be prevented. It would take more than that and the teaching of one art school to deflect the war that was looming, but Arthur Lismer remained convinced of the importance of the quality of teaching provided for the young. He was a crusader in painting and he was a crusader in teaching. It is not often that such richness is vouchsafed to one man.

NOTES

1 Arthur Lismer. "Art and the Average Canadian," *Canadian Courier*, February 1, 1919

2 Ken Johnstone. "The Professor is a Rebel," *New Liberty*, May 1951, pp. 32–33, 44–52

3 Marjorie Lismer Bridges. *A Border of Beauty.* Toronto: Red Rock Publishing Company Limited, 1977, p. 28

4 Arthur Lismer to Eric Brown, March 21, 1920, National Gallery of Canada

5 Brockville *Recorder and Times*, April 10, 1934

6 Arthur Lismer to Harry McCurry, September 16, 1929, National Gallery of Canada

7 Shirley Yanover. *The Gallery School 1930–1980: A Celebration.* Toronto: Art Gallery of Ontario, 1980, p. 9

8 Arthur Lismer. "The Canadian War Memorials," *The Rebel*, IV, no. 1 (October 1919), pp. 40–42

9 Arthur Lismer, "Children and Art," *Canadian Forum*, XVI, no. 4 (January 1936), pp. 12–15

10 S. Yanover. *The Gallery School*, p. 10

11 Michael Ballantyne. "Childhood and the World of Art," *Canadian Art*, XXI, no. 6 (November/December 1964), pp. 336–41

12 Arthur Lismer. "Children and Art," *Canadian Forum*.

13 Arthur Lismer. "The Value, Meaning and Place of Art in Education," *Dalhousie Review*, October 1928, pp. 378–389

14 Naomi Jackson Groves. *A.Y.'s Canada.* Toronto: Clarke, Irwin & Company Limited, 1968, p.110

15 Arthur Lismer. "Children and Art," *Canadian Forum*, XVI, no. 4 (January 1936), pp. 12–15

16 Arthur Lismer. "Canadian Art," *Canadian Theosophist*, V, no. 12 (February 5, 1925), pp. 177–179

Figure 72
Humberside Collegiate,
Toronto c.1928

CHAPTER SEVEN

The Humberside Mural

While Arthur Lismer was forging ahead with his work in child art, he was also busy with a mural commission, a much larger endeavour than the ones he had completed in Halifax. Murals were difficult to popularize at that time, for it was hard enough to find money for a building, let alone pay an artist to execute a mural. In 1894, George Reid and six other artists had formed the Society of Mural Decorators to promote the commissioning of murals in public buildings. Eventually the work of promotion began to bear fruit in the halls of Toronto's collegiate institutes.

Humberside Collegiate Institute had opened in 1894 with an enrolment of sixty-eight. The area served by the school was at that time just outside the city of Toronto; the district was known as the Junction since railroads converged there. But the old Belt Line that ran as far as the Humber River eventually fell into disuse and the three-cent Bloor trolleys that carried passengers from Dundas to Runnymede Road were replaced by long, shiny, showy cars that ran along the new viaduct built under the railway halfway between Lansdowne and Dundas. By the middle of the Roaring Twenties, Toronto had grown to encompass the Junction, and to accommodate the teenagers of the expanding city, an addition to Humberside Collegiate was opened in 1924.

The addition included an auditorium large enough to seat the whole school. The western wall was blank, and in 1925 the staff and literary society of the school decided to enhance it with a mural. Arthur Lismer, ARCA, member of the avant-garde Group of Seven and vice-principal of the Ontario College of Art, was chosen to design and execute it. No one knows what instructions, if any, were given to him about subject matter, but it was a foregone conclusion that the mural would not be dull.

As a result of recent publicity, mural commissions had become somewhat more popular, and inspired a certain amount of professional rivalry. That same year the Royal Canadian Academy sponsored a competition for a mural for the Earlscourt Public Library. First prize for design went to J.E.H. MacDonald for *A Friendly Meeting, Early Canada*. The Academy allotted a small sum for expenses, but otherwise the costs were borne by the artists who undertook the work under the direction of G.A. Reid, by now principal of the Ontario College of Art. Reid himself had already decorated the walls of the auditorium in Jarvis Collegiate. The murals there were executed in traditional mural manner in dark greens, blues and browns, and comprised a thorough job, for every inch of every wall in the auditorium was completely covered.

Figure 73
*The "allegorical" panel of the
Humberside mural*

A mural in Humberside Collegiate would have to accommodate itself to a wall that sported four nine-and-a-half-foot
panels divided by pillars and a fifth triangular space above the
balcony. In addition, because the literary society was raising
the money piecemeal, only one panel per year was to be
completed, a rather anti-climactic hurdle for an artist to overcome. As Lismer wrote later in the *Journal of the Royal
Architectural Institute of Canada*: "The painter and sculptor
resent the idea of being an 'also ran' contributor, a kind of
after-thought who will be employed only if there is enough
money left over to give him a show." And there was another
aspect to consider. "Most artists regard the decorator of wall
surfaces as rather an inferior member of the craft of painting, a
sort of workman who wields brushes and paints, certainly, but
who erects scaffolds and has to know about surfaces, areas,
mediums, scales, and so forth." Lismer himself regarded mural
painting as a challenge, for the mural painter,

> …must possess a different mental and spiritual equipment, a
> sense of orchestration and a powerful imagination … a nature that
> can rise above the objective and literal, and the ability to sacrifice
> mere personal caprice in the service of a bigger thing than himself.
>
> The ability to think, to visualize noble proportions, to project
> onto the surface of the wall a nobler, grander pattern of life than
> the fussy realism of the average subject picture is a prime essential
> of the art. [1]

The theme that Lismer would choose for his mural would be
inspirational, for education in the twenties was designed to
form character. It would be nationalistic, for the twenties
represented a peak in Canada's pride in her growing development, her membership in the great British Empire and her own
dominion that stretched from sea to sea. It would be optimistic, for that was Lismer's own nature. It would also be controlled to the last detail, for although Lismer liked to pass himself
off as happy-go-lucky, he was actually relentless in his insist-
ence on perfection.

He planned it carefully. The first panel put into place, the
middle one, was allegorical:

On a pleasant slope there are figures representing various attributes and ideals. The conception of Childhood is revealed amid pleasant flowers and foliage, with the rainbow, rosy colours, blossoms and birds. The mother represents devotion and care. The stream suggests the River of Life with turbulent passages and quiet pools; the young pine tree in the centre, the sturdy quality of a nation's youth. The little girl with the dove is Innocence, and the figure of the maiden, attended by the fawn, symbolic of woodland grace, is Beauty. Beside the path to the left, stands a pilgrim who represents Courage and the aspirations of Youth. He is gazing upward towards the mountains at the figure of Truth, which is the highest figure of all, above Courage, Beauty and Wisdom, above the tops of mountains radiant against the blue Zenith of the sky. High on her pinnacle, she looks serenely over the affairs of men. When the whole series is completed, she will still be the dominant and highest figure of all.

From the first the object has been to make this panel Canadian in spirit – that is: it is youthful and energetic; it is optimistic in colour and bright in tone.

The remaining panels would be different. They will not have the allegorical aspect of the centre one. To the left, against a background of sea, lake and bush, two panels will portray the contributions of the Old World and the New. The two panels at the right will represent Canadian achievement in Agriculture, Science, Letters and Art. Youth of the schools and universities with its hopes and ideals, physical prowess and mental energy, will find a place. The background will be of Canada today, with cities and farms, bridges and elevators. When the five panels are complete, Truth will still be the central figure, highest of all.[2]

The first panel was unveiled at the commencement exercises in the fall of 1928, and the last one in 1932, when the mural could finally be seen as a whole. It possessed a strange power. The colours were not the strong reds and greens of Lismer's northland paintings, nor the dull tones of many other murals of that time. They were the glowing, sunlit colours of the Impressionists, colours of springtime – soft blues, greens, yellows, tans, light browns, and pearly, unearthly shades of pink in the women's and children's dresses. The blending of the

colours was subtle but strong; the rise and fall of movement from one panel to another, both by colour and placement of figures, was masterly. The whole mural sparkled, was vibrant.

Here were the Vikings, emerging shadowy from time long ago. Here was Cabot, weary but satisfied; Cartier confident; Champlain, bright-eyed with plans for development; a coureur-de-bois, purposeful; an Indian brave with scalp-lock, strong, waiting; an Indian maiden, wondering; a priest and nun, watchful. Here were James Wolfe, frail but confident, and Isaac Brock in red coat and plumed hat, ready to charge boldly but fatally up Queenston Heights past a cannon camouflaged in stones and leaves. These two panels, represented the Old World. The two panels on the right of the central one represented the New World with a lumberman leaning on a peavey; immigrants from Europe; a boy with his dog and book representing the beginning of education; a mother, the maternal side – sustaining and nurturing growing life. A fifth panel, above and below the auditorium balcony, belonged to the future of aviation and science.

Lismer's Humberside mural contained figures that were large and impressive, but also individualized. The faces are as clear as portraits and every detail is natural. A young girl plays with a buckskin doll, an older boy reads a book. The dog has its ears cocked and its eyes are bright with the anticipation of play. The garb of the hunter is soft and pliant; the breeches of the courtier are plainly made of fine cloth. Wild irises grow beside the stream and trilliums bloom among the leaves and mossy logs. A frog sits on a lily pad.

The effect of the mural is strong and dramatic. To lend punctuation and drama to his galaxy of colours and figures, Lismer employed a deep, clear blue, the same blue he would use in *Bright Land*. A courtier's cloak on the left, a lumberman's shirt on the right, the mountain and the blue zenith of the sky are all drawn together by this distinctive, pulsating blue. None of the figures in the central panel received this dominant blue, reserved for the cathedral-like mountain and sky, against which is silhouetted the robed, high, central figure of Truth.

Lismer prepared the preliminary sketches for the mural in his Bedford Park studio, beginning with the central panel. The studio could accommodate the ten-foot width of the panel, but its eighteen-foot height was too much for the fifteen-foot ceiling. He hinged the framework three feet from the bottom and top. The canvas was a roll of raw Belgian linen weighing about three hundred and fifty pounds, brought from Austria with the Cizek Child Art exhibition. It was stretched on a frame, sealed with gelatin, then covered with off-white as a base. The $70 cost of the canvas for the first panel was borne by the Toronto Board of Education. The school literary society raised the money to pay the artist $400 per panel.

Whenever possible, Lismer consulted the Humberside staff and student committee. No detail was too small for his attention or jocular temperament. The principal of the school, John S. Wren, was acknowledged in the mural as a wren, and the head of the art department, Salem Bartholomew Hatch, as a nuthatch. Mr Hatch would be further immortalized: he was a fine-looking man with an old-fashioned walrus moustache and thick, curling gray hair; all that was needed to turn him into Wisdom was the addition of a Moses-beard.

When completed, the mural transcended the architectural limitations of the auditorium. Instead of stretching to the ceiling in a straight line, each panel was a different height, governed by a great curve that swept up from the Old World panels over the head of Truth and down to the panels of the future. "In the last 100 years," Lismer wrote, "the architect and painter have lost touch with each other, and both with the fundamental logic of architectonic character needed to give powerful expression to contemporary decoration.... There are signs that our democracy, which is still in its adolescence, is slowly achieving a new renaissance through more co-ordinated activity in the designing of structure and its decoration."[3]

Lismer's philosophy about the essential relationship of interior design to architecture would be reflected in the decoration of many subsequent public buildings, but it did not protect his own mural. Between 1966 and 1968, when the post-Second World War baby boom necessitated another addition to the collegiate, a larger auditorium was built and the old auditorium was turned into a library. The wall was needed for bookshelves. What was to happen to the mural?

Scrap the old-fashioned mural, was the attitude of the planners. Put a match to it. Tradition-conscious members of the teaching staff were horrified. That mural had been painted by a member of the Group of Seven, they said, and besides, the Board of Education did not own it. It belonged to the student body because they had paid for it.

After a fight initiated by outraged staff members Grace Irwin and Nora Belcher, the mural was saved, after a fashion. It was taken down, but had been so well affixed to the wall by a mixture of lead varnish and enamel that diamond dust had to be used to loosen it. The panels were rolled and stored by the Board of Education, then entrusted to William Michaud for cleaning and restoring. Michaud claims that this was the biggest restoration job in the history of Canadian art.

There was no wall in the new wing high enough to hold the restored mural. The only space available was the front wall of a tiered lecture hall, too low in the ceiling to cope with the full height of the mural and its great curve. The frieze was cut off the bottom of the highest panels and the end panels were raised so that they did not match the adjacent ones. Some of the unused pieces disappeared. Two of the missing sections have been located, one in private hands and the other in the care of the McMichael Canadian Collection in Kleinburg, Ontario, that was opened under provincial auspices in 1965 to house the achievements of the Group of Seven.

Lismer believed firmly in the role of art as a "visual and convincing manifestation of the Creator's purpose." He wrote: "We need vision, creative acts, poetry, inspiring music, and a picture of the land we fight for in peace and war. We need to be told over and over again that life can unfold like a symphony, as a tree grows, as the colours of the hills fade into infinity. We need to see painting as a visual and convincing manifestation of the Creator's purpose. The artist, if he is anything, is the interpreter of that purpose, creating out of idea, out of void, an unfolding plan, an echo, a shadow of the creative intention."[4]

The Humberside mural responded to the needs of a time when Canadians were acutely aware of the importance of their country's historical heritage and the responsibility to instill moral values in her youth. But as an artistic achievement, the Humberside mural holds its own as well, fulfilling a twofold purpose: "It is necessary that as Canadians we should believe that we are as capable of producing great art as we believe we are capable of doing great deeds."[5] This was written by the man who had accepted Canada as his own and put Canada in his mural.

NOTES

1 Arthur Lismer. "Mural Painting," *Journal of the Royal Architectural Institute of Canada*, x. no. 7 (July 1933), pp. 127–135
2 Humberside *Hermes*, 1929
3 Arthur Lismer. "Mural Painting"
4 Arthur Lismer. "A.Y. Jackson, LL.D., Painter of Canada: An Appreciation," January 30, 1942 (speech in manuscript), Art Gallery of Toronto
5 Arthur Lismer. "Canadian Art," *Canadian Theosophist*, v, no. 12 (February 15, 1925), pp. 177–179

Figure 74
The La Cloche Mountains,
Killarney

CHAPTER EIGHT

Bright Land

The twenties were productive if tumultuous years for Arthur Lismer. They witnessed the formation of the Group of Seven and the painting of magnificent landscapes like *A September Gale* in Georgian Bay, *Isles of Spruce* in Algoma and *Cathedral Mountain* in the Rockies. They saw the beginning of his work in child art and the production of the Humberside mural. They had also taken him in 1923 and 1929 to McGregor Bay and in 1933 Baie Fin, both in the southeastern part of the Algoma district. The thirties enticed Lismer back to McGregor Bay twice, in 1933 and 1935.

Near Killarney, Espanola and Whitefish Falls, there is a range known as La Cloche, so named by early Indians who had discovered that the rock rang like a bell when struck. This southeastern part of the District of Algoma differs in colouring from the area the Group had investigated in their boxcar trips. The distinctive quartzite and silica composition of the rock makes it marble-white in colour. Unlike the lower, rocky stretches of western Algoma, its hills are high enough to be called mountains.

Frank Carmichael had heard that there were mountains somewhere in northwestern Ontario, and in 1923 he went to find them. He traveled by canoe and foot to Cranberry Lake where he set up his tent. Later with Bud Hopkins, a guide from Whitefish Falls, he penetrated farther to Nellie Lake. Carmichael's *Light and Shadow* and *Hilltops* were painted nearby. Jackson's *Nellie Lake* was painted overlooking the southwest corner.

Lismer heard about the locality through Carmichael, and about McGregor Bay in particular from his friend Dr Arthur Bensley, a professor of biology at the University of Toronto who cottaged in the vicinity. Lismer was as eager for new scenes as Carmichael; but as his family preferred not to tent, he chose McGregor Bay where there was a cluster of about fifteen cottages, a general store and a dock.

Arriving at this pocket of civilization entailed taking the transcontinental train to Sudbury and the next morning boarding the Algoma Eastern that chugged from Little Current to Sudbury carrying lumber or ore. En route the train would pick up anyone who flagged it down, so by this point in the journey punctuality was relatively unattainable.

Lismer dubbed the train the "Agony Eastern." It had gas lights and woven straw seats so slippery that passengers had to hang on the the arms of their seats when rounding a curve. The curves were terrifying. The Pullman listed heavily to each side. At one particularly sharp turn, the passengers were eyeball to eyeball with the engineer. If the faint-hearted survived this

Figure 75
FRANK CARMICHAEL *n.d.*
pencil on paper
19.6 × 25.1 *cm*

awesome sight, there were still slopes to be surmounted as the engine laboured upwards. At crucial points Lismer would chant in time with the wheels, "I hope I can, I hope I can, I hope I can." Then, "I think I can, I think I can, I think I can." Finally, triumphantly, "I made it, I made it, I made it." He knew children's books as well as their art.

McGregor Bay juts into the south shore of Lake Huron east of North Channel and northwest of Georgian Bay. The settlement there was founded about 1910 when Stuart Jenkins, a graduate of McGill University and former editor of the Little Current *Expositor*, built a two-storey log house to get away from the frustrations that were causing his ulcers. The cottage that the Lismers rented was on an island a bit offshore from Jenkins's store.

Both the Jenkinses had definite ideas about what they admired in art. Mr Jenkins painted well and was an expert copyist; he used a dry brush and infinite care with his seascapes, though he was miles from the sea. They did not admire the style of the Group of Seven, and after dinner would argue with Lismer about art. Lismer, tall, slender and energetic, would stride up and down as he talked, gesticulating to prove his points. "Egad, sir," Mr Jenkins once said, adjusting his cuffs, "you can't draw or you wouldn't paint such blobs. A painter must be able to draw."

Lismer whipped out his ever-present pen. "I'll prove to you that I can draw." He drew a well-finished rock picture, perfect in line and truthful representation, but without the verve he delighted in. He gave it to Mr Jenkins. "Now when you frame it, promise me that neither the date nor the signature will show, for that is not the way I wish to be known."

Mr Jenkins accepted the drawing with pleasure. "Now, Mrs Jenkins," he said, with the argument ended to his satisfaction, "shall we have a cup of tea?"

When Lismer first holidayed in McGregor Bay, he was not yet known as a famous artist, and the name Hot Mush was still fresh in the air. Fame is not easily won. He once presented Stuart Jenkins's daughter Ethel with a painting, but she hid it in a closet and later gave it away as if it were a poisonous spider. By weighing the number of approving reports against the number of adverse ones, art historians may try to prove that

Figure 76
BRIGHT LAND (*sketch*)
oil on board
45.7 × 54.5 *cm*

Figure 77
LILIES AND APPLES 1931
oil on cardboard
30.7 × 40.5 *cm*

the Group members created their own myths about the opposition they faced. It is true that they enjoyed and benefited by the attention they were getting, but a tale at grassroots level can sometimes give a better idea than arithmetic of what they contended with.

The Lismers usually rowed to get out of the cottage area to a good painting spot. If someone was around to drive a three-and-a-half horsepower kicker, they had the convenience of a speedier conveyance, but Lismer himself never drove anything. It took an hour and a half to reach places like Hanging Rock where Lismer would leave his wife and daughter to read or knit while he clambered to a vantage spot. When his stomach signaled lunch time, he would slide down, light a fire to make fresh coffee and, finding a rock to sit on, arrange his long legs so that he could balance his plate. The usual pattern for a painting day was a picture in the morning, a sketch or two in the afternoon, and, if the light was special, another sketch in the evening.

If they wished to go farther afield than the kicker would take them, there was Jenkins's big boat. Off in the direction of Killarney was Old Baldy, its gleaming white marble contours laced with green pine. Lismer could sit on the ridge near Lake Josephine, on Iroquois Island, or on Sampson Island and without moving from one spot, produce a panorama of sketches as he looked in various directions.

Besides oils, he used black conté chalk, a Chinese brush and ink, a felt pen, or a fountain pen with black ink. He also used his own brand of home-made reed pen. These pens were made from a weed with a bamboo-like configuration of stem called Canadian bamboo, knotweed, or *polygonum cuspidatum*. Charlie Goldhamer, a former colleague of Lismer's, still keeps some in his South Kingsway garden, more for the memory of the many pens Lismer gave out to his students with a hearty recommendation for their use, than for any lingering love for what they might do for his drawing. These pens gave Lismer the rough expressive line he liked better than that which flowed from the smooth commercial pens.

Lismer once said to a McGregor Bay resident that it was in McGregor Bay that he found himself as a painter.[1] Certainly he had no difficulty now matching the force of the rocks against

Figure 78
MACGREGOR BAY 1933
ink on paper
30.5 × 38.1 *cm*

Figure 79
GEORGIAN BAY PINE *n.d.*
pen and ink on paper
22.9 × 17.8 cm

the weight of the sky and imbuing his canvases with a living quality that transcended mere technical skill. His friend, Barker Fairley, sensed this when he viewed the 1925 exhibition of the Group of Seven: "Lismer has made a great leap forward and painted his best pictures, *The Happy Isles* and *McGregor Bay*. The rest of the exhibition is flat."[2]

Perhaps it was not so much a great leap forward in expertise as a greater range of perception. He had already captured the great rhythms of the land by means of colour and form, lifting them so far out of the ordinary that they seemed a link with eternity. Harris was seeking to express eternity through ethereal light, but Lismer's sense of the everlasting came through a feeling for a life force.

This life force permeated every facet of flora and fauna, earth and water. Lismer's feeling for growth lent a drama and a vitality to whatever he painted. Storm or stillness, sun or shadow, rock or tree, every animate or inanimate thing vibrated for him, and his portrayals were as varied as his subjects.

He still looked into the distance, still encompassed a mighty scene, but now he was beginning to regard his subjects more closely, to see the trunks of trees instead of their entirety, to examine the undergrowth they rose from. Lismer said his Group friends stepped right over the foreground of their paintings as if it did not exist. He was beginning to enjoy making clarity out of the confusion of twisting roots and random growth, for in the foreground, right at his feet, was where life began. Mrs Charles Band once said that he was impelled to do this because clutter matched the exuberance of his nature.

In *Old Pine, McGregor Bay* (formerly *Pine Wreckage*) distance and vista are still there, but so is the struggle for the growth of each root and bush. Even the rocks do not seem inert. Another McGregor Bay painting, *Pine Wrack*, reveals something else. There is nothing art nouveau about Lismer's trees now. They derive their twisted strength from the ground; their roots clutch the rocks, struggling crookedly to send their tentacles deep. The boles of the trees wrench their living from the earth. Distance and light are now background, not an end in themselves. "The landscape painter," he said, "has to compose, to boil down as it were, his own optical impression to diminutive proportions and yet retain the quality and identity

Plate 21
BRIGHT LAND 1938
oil on canvas
81.1 × 101.5 *cm*

Plate 22
PINE RHYTHM 1947
oil on canvas
53.3 × 66 cm

Plate 23
ROCKY CHANNEL,
MACGREGOR BAY 1935
oil on board
54.6 × 66 cm

Plate 24
LITTLE LAKE, BAIE
FINN 1932
oil on canvas
66.7 × 81.5 cm

of the whole. His sketch becomes the unit as it were from which nature took its theme."[3] He had learned to read nature with nature's own eyes.

Interspersed between Lismer's visits to McGregor Bay in the twenties and early thirties were holidays at Georgian Bay, often with Charles Band and his family of four at their cottage on Rock-Lee Island. Mr Band was a major patron of the arts, a member of the education committee when Lismer was expanding his work at the Gallery, and president of the executive council on two later occasions. Mrs Band was one of the founders of the Gallery's women's committee in 1945.

In 1933 the Lismers traveled to La Cloche. There are three spurs to the La Cloche Mountains. One lies south of McGregor Bay and another north of Killarney. In between lies Baie Fin or Bay Fin, one of the most beautiful spots in the area. Baie Fin is long, narrow, and walled intermittently with white cliffs that stretch into the marbled distance. The Lismers rented a cottage on an island past the narrow entrance, and it was likely in Baie Fin that Lismer painted the sketch for *Bright Land*. In 1938, he enlarged and finished it. It is probably a composite of many of Lismer's beloved painting places in both the La Cloche and Georgian Bay regions.

After a sojourn at Baie Fin, they moved over to McGregor Bay, where Lismer painted until autumn's cold and colour came in the last days of August. When it was finally time to return to his teaching, Lismer's panels were no longer empty; they were filled with the essence of that bright land.

NOTES

1 Julia Botan (Stuart Jenkins's granddaughter) to Lois Darroch, July 1980
2 Barker Fairley. "The Group of Seven," *Canadian Forum*, v, no. 53 (February 1925), p. 144

Plate 25
PINE WRACK 1933
oil on canvas
92.1 × 106.9 cm

Figure 80
A South African landscape

CHAPTER NINE

Lismer Unlimited

The genre of landscape painting that came to a climax in *Bright Land* is only one facet of Arthur Lismer's work. The caricatures, studies, quiet Halifax paintings, the magnificent war drawings and murals are only five more. As early as 1930 Lismer produced watercolour and ink creations so sparing of detail and so striking in their use of blank space that they do not seem to belong to the artist who loved detail so much that every root and vine at the base of a tree, every stay on a mast, could pass a test for accuracy.

Harbour Scene, Halifax (1930) is a simple depiction of a wharf and harbour shed, part ink and part watercolour. In the foreground is a killick held in place by a stone as old as time and so strong it seems only a Hercules could budge it. Cabled ropes twine in front. The background has space, buildings merely outlined in ink and washed in carelessly, casting bluish shadows on blue water. A few squiggles of the brush, black on blank paper, suggestive of logs and building paraphernalia, complete the scene. In utter contrast to the Georgian Bay, Algonquin and Algoma oils, this painting is executed with the sparse strokes of Oriental calligraphy. Here is yet another facet of Lismer's variety and mastery.

He painted at Lunenburg, Peggy's Cove and Grand Manan Island as well as Halifax that summer. "The place is lousy with artists," he wrote about Grand Manan to Eric Brown.[1] Here he indulged his growing love of detail, this time massing ropes, lobster pots and fishing boats in organized complexity.

Whenever possible he took his family with him. He had been invited by Marius Barbeau and Alex Jackson to go to the Skeena country in British Columbia, but he declined, saying, "I prefer to go with my family." Instead, he sketched in Quebec at various times at Ile d'Orléans and Baie St Paul. But no matter what he painted, it was always full of vitality. His scenes were never plain. In *Quebec Village* (1926), he spiritualized the church with a tier of halos. A farmhouse against a sweep of landscape (*Farmhouse, Baie St. Paul*, 1925) was somehow given a mischievous look. The hens scratching around it were slightly un-hen-like, and a turkey who flaunted his fan nearby had a flamboyant air about him that no one else was likely to discern in a barn yard turkey. His friend and fellow artist in Montreal, Harold Beament, said of this tendency in Lismer's work: "There was a controlled rowdiness in Lismer, a roughness. His turbulence showed through his training – he had the ability to go beyond what his training had led him to."[2]

In the course of his search for fresh scenes to paint, Lismer also visited Lake Mazinaw northeast of Peterborough where Bon Echo rock loomed like a Canadian Gibraltar. Here Flora

Figure 81
HARBOUR SCENE 1930
ink and watercolour
35.6 × 44.5 cm

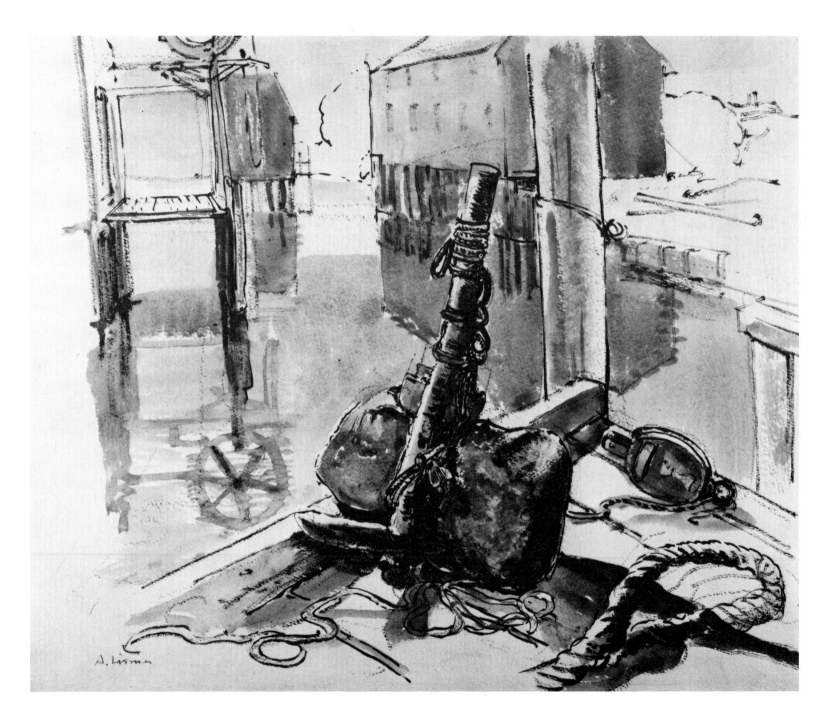

Figure 82
DERELICT PIER 1941
oil on canvas
55.3 × 66 cm

Figure 83
ROCKY HARBOUR *n.d.*
ink on paper
26.6 × 37.2 cm

MacDonald Denison held court in a fifteen-room hotel. Flora believed that early to bed and early to rise meant that one missed many interesting people and their activities. So she ran a resort for interesting people, preferably those who liked Walt Whitman and his democratic ideals. She engraved on Bon Echo rock in foot-high letters:

My foothold is tenon'd and mortised in granite.
I laugh at what you call dissolution
And I know the amplitude of time.

Flora's son, playwright Merrill Denison, was a member of the Arts and Letters Club, and a holiday at Bon Echo meant plenty of time for stimulating discussion as well as an opportunity to paint.

In 1919, Hart House was completed and presented to the University of Toronto in memory of Hart Massey. Just as the opening of the Art Gallery of Toronto in 1921 was considered a landmark event in the art world, so was Hart House a landmark in providing facilities for extra-curricular cultural activities at the University of Toronto. Vincent Massey had insisted that the building contain a 500-seat theatre. The first director was Roy Mitchell, member of the staff of the Ontario College of Art. One of the first presidents was Dr John Robins of

Figure 84
BARN, ILE D'ORLEANS 1925
reed-pen and black ink
31.8 × 37.3 cm

Figure 85
ON THE GATINEAU 1926
brush and ink on paper
27.9 × 38.1 cm

Victoria College, and among the actors were included Vincent Massey and his brother Raymond. Lismer and other members of the Group of Seven were enlisted as set designers.

The basement of University College provided the space for building the sets. Lismer, art director for a time, was adept at giving just enough advice to help people over hurdles, but not enough to kill initiative. When Carl Schaefer was having trouble with the two-wheeled Irish cart for *Hugh, the Drover,* Lismer drew a quick sketch on the concrete floor, and then went off. He came back later to check on progress, scribbled some more with the chalk, and left, trusting Carl and the others to finish the job.

In 1927, J. Murray Gibbon convinced the CPR that a series of folk festivals across Canada would promote passenger traffic and nationalism at the same time. Lismer designed the sets for a French folk festival at the Chateau Frontenac in Quebec City in 1927 and 1928, for a Scottish festival at Banff in 1928 and for an English one (*Hugh, the Drover*) in 1929 at the opening of the Royal York Hotel in Toronto.

As the thirties progressed, Lismer did what he could to alleviate the numbing weight of the Depression. Even before the Saturday classes took care of some of the children, he gathered students and unemployed into the Children's Art Centre one evening a week to project their work on a screen

Plate 26
DOCK LITTER C.1940
oil on canvas mounted on wood
40.6 × 50.8 cm

Plate 27
FISHING GEAR, CAPE
BRETON ISLAND 1940
watercolour on paper
30.5 × 45.7 cm

Plate 28
CAPE BRETON, NOVA
SCOTIA, NEAR
CHETICAMP 1939
oil on plywood
61 × 81.2 *cm*

and offer suggestions. He sent his best students to teach the unemployed in two little craft shops: one in the east end of the city and another in Barrie. It kept them busy. On some occasions Lismer himself paid the traveling expenses of a few students who were anxious to paint outside the city.

He was in the forefront of any organization that would further education or popular understanding of the arts. He gave enthusiastic support to the Canadian Association for Adult Education, presiding at the first national conference at Macdonald College in Guelph, in June 1935. This made him one of the pioneers in adult education. Later, in 1941, he was active with André Biéler in establishing the Federation of Canadian Artists at Kingston, an organization that was designed to help end the isolation of artists and to keep them abreast of new media and methods. He was a vocal and provocative participant on both the national and the Quebec regional committees of the Federation.

Lismer was now much in demand as a lecturer, for he was a pleasant, relaxed speaker who wanted people to enjoy themselves. With his long hair, already graying, he looked a trifle eccentric for the time. He lectured on art in education, industry and democracy, or gave straight lectures on art history and art appreciation. He talked about his work in child art.

Naturally he was questioned about Impressionism, still somewhat of a *bête noir* in certain art circles. Yes, he acknowledged freely, "Impressionism has left its mark on every country and every subsequent school of painting. Canadian painting has felt that influence."[3] Never at any time did he proselytize for the landscape art of the Group of Seven. People could draw their own conclusions.

It has been said that MacDonald visualized the Group of Seven movement and Harris materialized it or brought it into being. Lismer was the evangelist for Canadian art. He talked to business about its responsibility toward art. He told people how to acquire loans of reproductions and slides. Because of him, many a small-town art association was organized and its members inspired to do more than copy existing paintings. Take a little book and sketch every day, he told them.

His success as a lecturer induced the National Gallery to send him on a tour to the west in the spring of 1932. In July he

Plate 29
THE BIG ROCK, BON ECHO 1922
oil on canvas
91.6 × 101.7 cm

was off again, this time to France where he attended a world conference of the New Education Fellowship in Nice and met international educators like John Dewey. All were fascinated by his lectures on "Art in a Changing World," and by the exhibition of child art he took with him. After the conference, he led an art appreciation tour of galleries in Venice, Florence, Rome and Paris.

In particular South African educators at the conference recognized that Lismer's work in child art was one of the most significant things being done in education anywhere in the world. In the summer of 1933, the year in which the Canadian Group of Painters held its first showing, Dr E.G. Malherbe, the organizing secretary of the New Education Fellowship, invited Lismer to lecture the following year at Cape Town and Johannesburg at other NEF conferences.

Malherbe extended the invitation because he said South Africans were an art-starved people and he felt that Lismer's methods liberated an urge for creative expression in the souls and through the hands of ordinary school children. He had seen Lismer hold street boys as enthralled with his words and sketches as if they were listening to a detective thriller. Lismer's teachings might help cure some of the malaise that affected South African life at that time.

It was a major opportunity for Lismer to enhance both his and Canada's reputation. It also represented a major expense, and Lismer wrote to Eric Brown, asking if he could wangle something from somewhere, emphasizing that if he accepted the invitation he would take his family with him.[4]

He arrived in Cape Town for the New Education Fellowship Conference in July 1934. "Child art and adult art are two different concepts of life," he said in a lecture, "and we miss the real character of what the child reaches out for and how he says it if we compare this free expression of the child, unconscious and alive to rhythm and movement, with the conscious, historically and technically cultured adult. The child is closer to the native, the hunter-artist, and to prehistoric man as artist, than he is to the professional artist of today. He is sometimes a primitive, often poetic, and strangely lyrical, but always alive to the world around, for he is trying, as far as grown-ups will let him, to make a more harmonious place for his soul."[5]

He was given a gallery in the technical school in Cape Town for his display of child art. He emphasized that these pictures had not been done as school projects, but under the auspices of the Art Gallery of Toronto where children attended on a voluntary basis and were supplied with free materials. There, he said, they had freedom under disciplinary control. The display made so deep an impression on his audience that later a group of members of the Pretoria Parents' Association began to work for a Children's Art Centre, the first in the Union of South Africa. Soon it opened humbly on the top floor of the old Gymnasium School at Bosman and Poes streets. In 1941, only eight years after Lismer's visit, the centre moved into a fine new building on Skinner Street and in 1944, the Transvaal Education Department took over and expanded the centre for use in connection with its Teacher Training College.

South Africa was an exhilarating experience until it was time to return to Ontario where he had recently been turned down by the Royal Canadian Academy for full membership and where he was just ordinary Arthur Lismer, educational supervisor at the Art Gallery of Toronto. He commented wryly on this to Brown: "I have an idea I was thoroughly spoilt in South Africa – nobody is hanging on my shirt tail in this country."[6]

Never mind Ontario. He now had international renown. The result of this first short visit to South Africa was that he was invited to return there for a full year as educational consultant. Again the Carnegie Corporation of New York subsidized his traveling expenses; his salary was to be paid by three of the four provinces of South Africa.

As the flurry of preparation for his "South African Expeditionary Force" was coming to an end, he wrote again to Brown: "Leaving for South Africa on the Empress of Australia, then Carnarvon Castle from Southhampton, June 10. I feel as though I were launching into space. I don't know what is ahead and what will be here when I come back. I only know that I have had so many parties that I am emotionally dehydrated and I shall be glad to get on a boat without a telephone or lecture. Au 'voir."[7]

Crowds of teachers and children went to see him off. It was a big occasion – who else was traveling at the height of the Depression? On this trip Lismer took watercolours with him, for this medium absorbed only the immediate time of an artist.

Figure 86
AFRICAN HUT, SOUTH
AFRICA *c.*1935
charcoal on paper
21.5 × 33 *cm*

Figure 87
SKETCH OF ELEPHANTS,
PENGUINS, MONKEYS
AND BIRDS *n.d.*
ink drawing
16.3 × 13 *cm*

Conscientious as usual, he knew he must concentrate on the teaching task for which he was being invited.

Lismer did not stay solely in the South African cities. He went to Basutoland, Zululand and Bechuanaland, staying in missions and native houses, driving over vast plains and hearing the calls of strange birds and animals at night. In remote villages he led "artistic orgies," encouraging people to show off their skills in the use of native materials and designs, giving them pride in their work instead of comparing it with foreign artifacts.

Sometimes he spoke in buildings, sometimes outside under the trees. Always he wanted the children to draw and paint for him. Once, when visiting a native school, he told them the story of Jack and the Beanstalk. He asked permission to draw on a whitewashed wall and there appeared a giant beanstalk that reached to the roof. Way down near the ground he drew a native hut and the distant mountains of their own land. They laughed with pleasure and Lismer wrote later, "I guess *that* wall has not been re-whitewashed since that day."[8] Now he could say from personal experience that the nature of children is the same all over the world.

Lismer wanted every child to have the same opportunities that Canadian children were beginning to have, but he was not blind to the social and political unrest in South Africa. There were two million whites and thirteen million natives and Asiatics. As he drew up his program for art in the schools, he wondered if it would be used in white schools only.

Whenever he could, he took out his watercolours to paint the African landscape with its orange overtones and blue and purple undertones. "In Africa, they don't enjoy the landscape," he noted in a radio broadcast later, "it is too dangerous."[9] He painted the people with their deep-toned skin.

"South Africa was the richest experience of my life," he said in an interview in Montreal. "It took me to the native territories, to the native villages, and I worked with very simple people who had a direct view on life…it was rich beyond dreams, and I still think of the simplicity and the beauty and the vastness of the territory and the friendly reception we had on all sides.… I find that primitive people derive the greatest satisfaction and enjoyment out of their art and skills."[10]

Before he left, Lismer wrote comprehensive reports about what could be done to improve art education. The South Africans wished to continue the work that he had inspired, and he recommended that his Canadian assistant, Norah McCullough, be asked to head up the work. This she did, establishing the centre in Pretoria and other centres later in Cape Town and elsewhere through Cape Colony.

In the meantime, the Lismer family traveled home via Australia where there was another New Education Fellowship Conference. Lismer had been on the international executive for several years. They visited New Zealand, then returned to Canada, where Lismer's position at the Art Gallery of Toronto as educational supervisor had been held open for him. Yet he would not slide back surreptitiously into harness. He would still electrify the children, particularly an eleven-year-old named James Houston, who described this incident later:

> One morning, at the Gallery, a teacher announced that Arthur Lismer, who was just back from a trip to West Africa, was coming to see the children.
>
> All of a sudden we heard BOOM BOOM BOOM BOOM BOOM...*tremendous* African drumming...and this guy's about six foot four with this big tall dome of a head, and he's wearing this *huge* West African mask, and he comes in *banging* the drum and *dancing* and I don't know what it did to the other kids, but I nearly died. I thought *wow* – I mean, that's *it*! I just thought, – oh my God, you could go out to far places...and he's come from *Africa*...think of it!...and these people are making just the right kind of masks... You see, until then I hadn't connected my art world with my other world, especially Indians. But here was Lismer, tying it all together for me...the Indians, the Africans, the masks, the art... I just went wild![11]

Years later, James Houston would encourage the Eskimos of Cape Dorset, Baffin Island, to develop their own art ways.

Of course Lismer was interviewed after his return from South Africa. He said he was now convinced that Canada was the first of the dominions in art. Others were still under English influence, but because Canada was closer to London than the others, it had less respect for it, less nostalgia.

As the Depression tightened its hold on the country, many educational services were curtailed. The funding by the Carnegie Corporation had done its work and was discontinued in 1939. Lismer, sitting up late at night, juggling financial reports and requests for teaching materials, found no solution for the necessary financial cutback but to offer to resign as educational supervisor of the Art Gallery so that existing programs could be maintained. The staff members prepared to continue by themselves. But they felt the lack of his presence. As Dorothy Medhurst said, "What you didn't have was the tremendous unifying influence of a superb person."[12]

The National Gallery made tentative overtures to him to work with them, but there was the usual lag in decision-making attendant on such a large institution. In July, he attended a meeting of the New Education Fellowship in Honolulu, and on his return he resigned from his work at the Art Gallery of Toronto.

Lismer's livelihood was rescued by an invitation to become visting professor of fine arts, specializing in child art, at the Teachers College of Columbia University. Since he had no university degree to qualify him for the post, the proposition amused him somewhat. It also perplexed him, for it posed the perennial Canadian problem of whether to move to the United States for greater opportunities. Although he had resisted temptation to leave the country before, now his situation was different. The Group of Seven was recognized, his work with children was established, his reputation was international, and the opportunity to live in New York, the hub of the English-speaking world, was undeniably attractive.

He departed from Toronto's artistic puddle with mixed feelings. On August 28, 1938, he wrote to Harry McCurry, assistant director at the National Gallery:

> I have my appointment authenticated from Columbia and I thought they would let me through all right, but they don't guarantee it at the border – so I'm taking out immigration papers so that *if I stay*, I can get naturalized without any trouble later.... Marjorie [who had graduated in 1935 with an Honours degree in English and History from Victoria College, University of Toronto] goes with us, entered as a student at Columbia for a degree in anthropology.... I am already beginning to feel like an alien.[13]

His natural curiosity sustained him in the new position. He went to Harlem, visiting art centres where blacks gathered to indulge their cultural interests. He learned that "swing" was not just aimless unbridled movement, but rhythm incarnate.

Lismer stayed only for the year of his appointment. He did not care for New York's frenetic atmosphere. "The people ...don't let the world go by and enjoy it. They go by the world and wait for it to catch up." He wrote a comprehensive report on the state of education in New York, but he was afraid it would be pigeon-holed. The American passion for statistics appalled him: "They *know* so darned much about more and more, and they feel so little about less and less. I want to get my pick into their statistical exteriors and find the real man inside.... These people know so much about how the mind works that they do not stop to contemplate what it works *on.*"[14]

During his absence, the position in Ottawa had been confirmed, and now he could return to Canada at Brown's invitation to work under the aegis of the National Gallery and help bring into reality his and Brown's dream of a national art program for Canada. After a brief vacation at Cape Cod and Georgian Bay, he moved to Ottawa as head of the educational program sponsored by the National Gallery, and in March of 1940, he set out on a cross-Canada lecture tour.

He told his audiences that schools should have documentary visual libraries, not just a few art books, and that Canadian artists would have to come out of their ivory towers if they were to survive. They must engage in the struggle for democracy by painting scenes of everyday life. Art, along with everything else in a democracy, was being fought for in the Second World War, and art would live long after the wars, oppressions and dictators were forgotten.

The rest of the national education program was never implemented. Formal Eric Brown, so unlike breezy Arthur Lismer in demeanour, but so similar in initiative and perception, died in April 1939, before Lismer arrived in Ottawa; and in September 1939, Canada entered the Second World War. Even in peacetime, being an activist in Ottawa is like swimming through molasses, and the atmosphere of wartime was not conducive to maintaining a robust national art program. Lismer chafed at the inevitable delays of civil service methods. He called Ottawa "a place of bowler hats and Honey Dew intrigues" and his own position there one of "amiable insecurity."

But he hated war, and nowhere was the war more evident than in Ottawa. "Then I wonder why we have war. If people were busy creating things they would have no time for destruction and hatred – and we should not indoctrinate for anything, but let human beings grow naturally – in a land where the chief

Plate 30
THE BOAT DECK 1933
oil on canvas
63.5 × 76.2 cm

Plate 31
FALSE BAY, CAPE OF GOOD
HOPE 1938
*graphite and watercolour on
paper*
39 × 57.9 cm

Plate 32
MOCHUDI, BECHUANA
VILLAGE 1936
oil on panel
31 × 40 cm

Plate 33
POTS OF FLOWERS 1938
watercolour
33 × 50.8 cm

vital nourishment is their sustaining and natural art."[15] Alas for ideals pitted against a goose-stepping army.

Although he was at a crisis now with regard to employment, his paintings were becoming better known. He had had a successful individual showing in Montreal at the Scott Gallery in November of 1936, while he was in South Africa. His large canvases, such as *A September Gale*, were constantly on loan from the National Gallery. Although he had complained at times about the difficulty of combining teaching and painting, he had managed to do both.

Once again the way opened before him when the Montreal Art Association (now the Montreal Museum of Fine Arts) invited him to become its supervisor of education. The Carnegie Corporation was supplying funds and the possibility of founding another child art centre was too attractive a prospect for him to refuse.

In late 1940, at the age of fifty-five, Arthur Lismer put his hat on his foot, kicked it onto his head to sit at its usual cock-eyed angle, stuck his ever-present pipe in the corner of his mouth and set off for his new position. "You don't choose this job," he said with a healthy confidence in his own past achievements and future capability, "it chooses you."

NOTES

1 Arthur Lismer to Eric Brown, August 14, 1930, National Gallery of Canada

2 Harold Beament to Lois Darroch, March 20, 1976

3 Toronto *Evening Telegram*, January 10, 1933

4 Arthur Lismer to Eric Brown, May 26 and June 13, 1933, National Gallery of Canada

5 Arthur Lismer. "Exhibitions of Child Art at the New Education Fellowship Conference," July 1934, p. 1

6 Arthur Lismer to Eric Brown, November 1, 1934, National Gallery of Canada

7 Arthur Lismer to Eric Brown, May 26, 1936, National Gallery of Canada

8 Marjorie Lismer Bridges. *A Border of Beauty.* Toronto: Red Rock Publishing Company Limited, 1977, p. 36

9 "Voice of the Pioneer," CBC radio broadcast, March–April 1964

10 Undelivered interview for CBC radio, no date

11 Charles Taylor. *Six Journeys: A Canadian Pattern.* Toronto: House of Anansi Press Limited, 1977, pp. 80, 81

12 Shirley Yanover. *The Gallery School 1930–1980: A Celebration.* Toronto: Art Gallery of Ontario, 1980, p. 23

13 Arthur Lismer to Harry McCurry, August 28, 1938, National Gallery correspondence, National Gallery of Canada

14 Marjorie Lismer Bridges. *A Border of Beauty*, p. 45

15 *Ibid.*, p. 49

Figure 88
Montreal 1941

CHAPTER TEN

Montreal

Once again the world was Lismer's walnut ready to be cracked for its kernel, and Montreal in the forties was not a bad place to be. At that time it was the cultural capital of Canada: poetry was flourishing in the form of magazines like *Preview*, there was fiction from Hugh MacLennan and Gabrielle Roy, and there was "working class" art with Louis Muhlstock and abstract art with Fritz Brandtner.

There had already been some groundwork in child art. Dr Norman Bethune had gathered children into his apartment for painting sessions during the Depression. Fritz Brandtner and Marion Scott had tutored children in an attic room. Then Anne Savage, after being amazed at the sight of the children in the Art Gallery of Toronto, began Saturday morning classes at the Montreal Museum of Fine Arts in 1937.

There were no kindergartens in Montreal schools when Lismer arrived. He began classes at the Museum for three-year-olds for an hour and a half three times a week and four-year-olds for a whole morning if they were considered ready for it. They had free run of the Museum as long as they didn't touch, or get caught sliding down the banisters. Older children came after school for painting on Tuesdays, drawing on Thursdays, and modeling on Saturday mornings.

The children had never met anyone like Lismer. He made them feel as if they were his equals. "How good he made us feel," one said. When given the choice of going to the Santa Claus parade or to Saturday morning class, more than one child chose the art class.

As he built up enrolment and enlarged his staff, Lismer again organized group projects and pageants on themes Biblical, historic, South African or South Pacific. As enrolment outstripped the space in the Museum itself, new quarters became necessary. In 1946, Lismer opened the Children's Art Centre in a house behind the Museum that was part of its property. Its rooms soon pulsated with the squirming, absorbed little bodies as they wielded their big brushes on big sheets of paper. It was their own special place.

Lismer loved every moment of what he was doing. He would come bombing into class, his hair flying out from under his hat, fling the hat in one corner and his coat in another. He rarely sat or settled permanently, although he considered himself quite a quiet person, when teaching or otherwise:

I don't teach them, I just stand in the background, never interfering, and encourage them to express themselves creatively rather than correctly, line for line.

Little children grow through their art as well as their

Figure 89
Arthur Lismer with students at
the Children's Art Centre,
Montreal

intelligence. Our aims are...not to make artists or to teach skills
but to find out the personality of growing men and women....
The responsibility of the teacher of art is affection, service, if you
like, to give, not to intrude, to respect the child's idea and not to
insist on your own...give guidance without interference.... A
child is always mature for his particular level.... There is a kind of
beneficent contagion that has gone out from these children's classes that has helped to shape the new idea of education through art
in the country...and [he could never resist a chance to pun] the
child can enjoy himself to his art's content.[1]

So the "beneficent contagion" continued to spread under his
guidance. In 1955, the Montreal Museum honoured him with
an exhibition of child art done at the Children's Art Centre.
Reviewers called it spectacular.

In 1942, Lismer was appointed principal of the School of Art of the Montreal Art Association. If he was easy in his guidance of the young children, he could be relentless in his demands of older students, and some of his assignments were eccentric.

He taught all ages. He gave serious advice to one class of young ladies: "If you wish to continue with your art, marry someone who is able to support you." There were classes for older women seeking to indulge an interest long delayed. "A lot of ladies have their artist-grandfathers' miniatures at home. Some frightful things come of this, but they enjoy it." He went on with a twinkling eye to an interviewer from a Montreal paper, "My wife gets very jealous of the older ladies in my class, you know."

Lismer inaugurated amateur nights as well as classes, and here he was in his element. "Come on, come on," he would say to a reluctant candidate, "try your hand. You can't be any worse than the others!" Then he would pause beside an easel. "By the way, which model are you drawing?" Or stop beside one with a hideous sculptured head in front of him. "Self portrait, I presume?"[2] If the criticism was sometimes blunt, a word of praise was cherished, and so were the innumerable sketches that Lismer would draw with no more strokes than it took to write his name. He gave them away with customary prodigality.

As a result of his principalship Lismer could announce at an annual meeting in 1964 that 4,500 had taken classes at the Montreal Museum of Fine Arts and 630 annually were enrolled in the combined programs, taxing facilities to the utmost. He had done all this from the time he began with fifty students and no staff.

For the second time in his career he was teaching in a world at war. When he went to Vancouver to lecture, for he still lectured frequently, he found that the Vancouver Art Gallery was discontinuing its child art classes. War or no war, he told them, if we cut back now, we are not giving our children the education they deserve. Life was not so serious, however, that he could not find time to visit the Vancouver zoo. The dignity of the ducks and penguins amused him.

During holidays, he went to Halifax to paint and sketch naval and coastal defences. On several occasions he was accompanied by Donald C. Mackay who had attended Lismer's

Figure 90
CAR, GULL, FISH,
DIVER *n.d.*
watercolour
26.6 × 16.5 cm

extension classes at the University of Toronto and then taught child and adult classes at the Art Gallery. Mackay was with Lismer one day as the patrol boat brought them back from McNab's Island. He described the sight of the arrival of a ship loaded with young "war guests" from the British Isles:

> The Cunard liner *Britannic* [later sunk in the Mediterranean], carrying hundreds of British children evacuated from the bombed areas, came alongside. Arthur bought a large bagful of chocolate bars and tossed them up to the open decks, crowded with children, many of whom had chocolate for the first time. He kept up a shouted conversation, telling them he hoped they would enjoy Australia and to keep their eyes open to see the first kangaroos. Meanwhile, he made quick sketches of the bright little faces shouting, "You can't fool us. We're in Canada!"[3]

Lismer kept up his acquaintance with his former Group friends whenever possible. Jackson was in and about Montreal, peripatetic as ever. Fred Varley also lived in Montreal for a time, but disillusioned by one war, then the Depression, then another war, Varley had soured on life. After the success of his First World War paintings and portraits, he refused to return to "menial" commercial work. He hoboed about, claiming that the world owed him a living. Lismer said that the world did owe him a living, as well as thousands of dollars that he deserved but had never received for his paintings. He and others found portrait commissions for Varley whenever they could.

Lismer was perspicacious enough to realize that the landscape art of the Group of Seven was now "old hat" in a changing world, and he knew that he himself should change with it. Lismer's earlier works in Canada had often shown immense expanses of sky over small stretches of land and water; then the land had grown in power until it matched the weight of the sky, and he balanced rocks, trees, water and sky. His later work showed the sky pushed into ever lessening importance until it disappeared almost entirely with his increasing interest in the foreground.

Now, in Montreal, he essayed still lifes, a radical departure

Figure 91
INGONISH 1945
drybrush and ink on paper
43.8 × 58.7 *cm*

Figure 92
KILLICK PARADE 1945
brush and ink on paper
29.8 × 45.7 cm

Figure 93
BEACH STUDIES I (*from the artist's sketchbook*) c.1951
charcoal on paper
22.4 × 29.8 cm

for him. Some would say these paintings were after the manner of Cézanne. Certainly they were brilliant in colour, but they were too lively to be imitative. The name "still life" belied itself when applied to Lismer's versions. Plants in *Still Life* pulsated with life, writhing Medusa-like. A plate was placed as if it were ready to fall out of the frame. The vibrant colours exuded vitality, and so did the objects on the canvas. An apple appeared ready to career into space at any moment, and a daffodil in one corner reached out to the fruit on the plate as if ready to trumpet a challenge or crack a joke.

The shells in *Shell Design* (1944) were gay to the point of speaking. In other works in the same genre, objects are only half recognizable. An eccentric flower container would somehow be contoured with an owl's eye and beak, or a rock would be so endowed that prehistoric shapes seemed alive within it. There was always some jocular surprise. At first glance some of these still lifes appear so casual as to be careless, but in fact every line, every change of colour has meaning, often subtle to the point of abstraction. The seaside still lifes employ soft, elusive shades. The indoor ones usually show blatant primary colours. These were the paintings of the man who had said two decades earlier to a class that "A painting should be so organized that you can walk into the middle, sit down and reflect and then walk out again."

With these still lifes, Arthur Lismer proved that he could change his style, although his work was conservative when compared with that of many other artists. In 1948, the Montreal art world exploded with the famous Refus global (Total Refusal) manifesto of the Automatistes, a group of painters, including Gauvreau, Ferron and Borduas, who rebelled not only against the shackles of current painting styles, but also against church, state and existing morality. They made the Group of Seven's 1920 avowal seem like porridge in comparison.

But Lismer was not a man to be frightened by an explosion. He had helped to start one himself. He would never be an abstractionist, but he was deadly serious about the right of others to be as abstract as they wished:

> An abstract can be the essence of a multiplicity of forms abstracted or extracted for the purpose of expressing the point of view of the artist.... You have to grant an artist a personal vision, but he's not getting it from the past, he's getting it from inside. It's an inner vision, therefore he reduces it to the common denominator which is line, tone, colour, a lot of abstract words.

"Art often shocks us," he continued in a radio interview, because "it comes upon us as a blow to our preconceived notions of what the artist should have done to please us.... A shock is good for us sometimes."[4]

As the forties gave way to the fifties, there was another type of eruption in the Montreal art world. On opening night of the 1951 spring art exhibition at the Montreal Museum, the usual well-dressed, respectable crowd was circulating when suddenly a jeans-encased file of young protestors appeared to proclaim that their particular brand of art was being slighted. One of the respectable ones turned to Lismer. "Shocking!" he spluttered. Lismer fixed his sharp blue eyes on him and snapped, "Not at all. When people feel strongly about art, they are proving that it is, in fact, alive. Where there's revolt there's life.... And what is more piquant, the revolt is against the revolutionaries. Our modernists, men like Pellan, Borduas, de Tonnancour, are 'old hat' to these people leading today's revolt. I can sympathize with both sides, for it was not long ago that the Group of Seven were regarded as 'old hat' by the modernists. But there's nothing wrong with that. What is wrong is when people stop feeling strongly about things. Then decay has arrived."[5]

He knew that what he was witnessing was history in the making. One biographer has summarized Lismer's attitude to change: "Lismer was, after all, one of the most revolutionary of the Group, one of the most impatient with mere convention. But Lismer's opposition was to the shackles which men made of the traditions, not to the traditions themselves."[6]

Now that he was in his late fifties, principal of a large and flourishing art school and painter of many fine canvases, he was becoming something of a lion in the art world. Although an art-buying public – a public buying Canadian art – had still to be created in Canada, the situation was changing fast. One result for Lismer was that *Cathedral Mountain* found a permanent home. In 1955, it was bought by Blair Laing of the Laing Galleries in Toronto, along with several other Lismer paintings; a few years later the painting was returned to the Montreal Museum of Fine Arts in exchange for *Tugs in Halifax Harbour*.

Lismer was pleased that at last he was receiving due recognition as a painter, for his reputation as a teacher had somewhat overshadowed his other talent. He was still overly modest about his achievements. If someone said, "I love this sketch," he might jest, "There must be something wrong with you if you do. Here, take it." Now he began to be shown more often by Montreal dealers.

When his paintings were being shown in a commercial gallery, Lismer liked to appear unexpectedly. On one occasion in Montreal, he came in just as a client was about to buy. The proprietor had just told her where it was painted, that it was a very fine Lismer, and so on. Then he introduced the artist. "You like it? Why it's terrible. See, it should have been done like this, or this," he said gleefully, chuckling at the dismay on the dealer's face. It was no use being furious with him. He knew the painting would sell, and that if a buyer had no more mind of his own than to be swayed so easily, he was not the

Figure 94
Arthur Lismer in his office at the Montreal Museum of Fine Arts

right owner for one of his paintings anyway.

In 1946, Lismer was elected a full member of the Royal Canadian Academy. When Beament, who had also been elected a full member that year, phoned to congratulate him, Lismer said bluntly that it was about time. "Do you know how long I've waited to get off the Associate list? Twenty-seven bloody years." In 1951, Lismer was elected to the council, the governing body of the Academy.

Now that he was somewhat famous, radio and televison impinged upon Lismer's private world. He gave his first radio broadcast early in 1930 and his first telecast in 1950. He rather enjoyed the publicity after so many years, but one broadcast in particular annoyed him. The broadcaster had concocted dramatized bits that included "conversations with my mother in Yorkshire dialect and with my dear wife (this made her furious) which are totally out of key.... Why can't radio writers be just simple and direct? I hope nobody hears it." When the script was submitted to him for approval, he wrote beside a particularly saccharine section, "My wife thinks this is just goofy."[7]

Gone was the obscurity of the early Group days and their gardens in Thornhill. Now Lismer often had to guard his privacy, although his friends were always welcome. One winter evening Donald Mackay, visiting from Halifax where he was now director of the School of Art and Design, was invited to dinner:

> While Mrs Lismer was busy preparing it, Arthur was showing me some recent sketches. Ultimately Esther came in and said, 'I can't understand what happened to the broccoli. It has just disappeared.' Arthur pointed and there in the corner of the studio was a strong square of cardboard with broccoli standing upright, thumb-tacked into position to form a winding avenue of trees. He had made a spirited sketch in conté.[8]

Throughout the years, Esther had remained Lismer's helpmeet, remembering everything he forgot, the perfect reflector of his vitality. Through the critical storms and controversies, northern excursions, many moves and world travels, they remained a devoted couple. In a changing world, they themselves were stable.

Plate 34
THE BLUE BOAT, NEIL'S
HARBOUR, CAPE
BRETON 1945
oil on board
50.8 × 61 cm

Plate 35
SEA SHELLS, N.S. *c.*1932
oil on panel
15.9 × 22.9 cm

Plate 36
STILL LIFE 1951
oil on canvas
54.9 × 76.5 cm

NOTES

1 Joan Capreol, "Lismer Going Strong at 78," Toronto *Globe and Mail*, November 15, 1963
2 Montreal *Gazette*, January 27, 1955
3 Donald C. Mackay to Lois Darroch, August 25, 1976
4 Ken Johnstone. "The Professor is a Rebel," *New Liberty*, May, 1951, pp. 32–33, 44–52
5 Undelivered interview for CBC radio, no date
6 John A.B. McLeish. *September Gale: A Study of Arthur Lismer.* Toronto: J.M. Dent and Sons Ltd., 1955, p. 34
7 Marjorie Lismer Bridges. *A Border of Beauty.* Toronto: Red Rock Publishing Company Limited, 1977, p. 103
8 Donald C. Mackay to Lois Darroch, August 25, 1976

Figure 95
Lismer Bay, Vancouver Island

CHAPTER ELEVEN

Laissez Passer

In 1950, Arthur Lismer was accorded a retrospective exhibition that was shown at both the Art Gallery of Toronto and the National Gallery in Ottawa, where attendance reached fifteen thousand people. One hundred and five paintings and drawings were chosen to represent his mastery of colour, design and theme. Here were the early competent Georgian Bay paintings, and *The Guide's Home, Algonquin* that had captured spring in Algonquin Park. Here were the great rhythmic works of the soaring twenties: *A September Gale – Georgian Bay, September Sunlight, The Happy Isles, Rain in the North Country, Isles of Spruce, Sombre Isle of Pic – Lake Superior.* And here were the deep struggles of the McGregor Bay trees, the majesty of *Cathedral Mountain*, the valour of *Bright Land* and the South African watercolours. When Lismer attended, he ranged around the rooms as excited as a child. "I must look at them all. I haven't seen some of them for forty years," he said.[1]

A retrospective meant recognition, but it did not mean the end. He had still another part of Canada to paint. The following year he holidayed on Vancouver Island, exploring Galiano and Pender islands and spending three nights at a lodge at Wickaninnish Bay, Long Beach, in that part of the western coast of the island that is now Pacific Rim National Park.

He would return to this spot for sixteen summers. He was sixty-five years old. Would this change of scenery affect him in any way? Could you teach an old dog new tricks? What could anyone do in the country that Emily Carr had made her own?

Emily Carr had been on painting expeditions into the British Columbia forest since her first trip in 1911. The Group of Seven had had each other for company and sustaining fervour when they set out a few years later to traverse Canada; Emily Carr had gone alone with only her little dogs as companions in the strangeness. The Group had traveled safely in sportsman's canoe or by boxcar. She had braved the ocean waves in Indian crafts. Without roughing in an individual leaf, wave or cloud, she had learned to express on canvas the whole overwhelming force of forest, sea and sky. It was Marius Barbeau and Lawren Harris who saw her work and told Eric Brown about it. In 1927, she traveled east to see her pictures hung in an exhibition of West Coast art in Ottawa, and in Toronto she met the Group of Seven. "God bless the Group of Seven," she said fervently, because of the recognition and inspiration she drew from them.[2] In 1930, she was invited to exhibit with the Group and a little later with the Canadian Group of Painters. She was no longer working alone.

Arthur Lismer could not resist the temptation to draw the plump little woman who came east in 1927 to meet the rest of

Figure 96
Arthur Lismer in front of self-portrait

Figure 97
Arthur Lismer speaking to guests at his retrospective in 1950 at the Art Gallery of Toronto

the Group of Seven and view her own show at the National Gallery. On her second trip east in 1930 when she ventured to New York, he saw that she viewed Kandinsky and Braque and introduced her to Georgia O'Keefe and her husband Alfred Stieglitz. On his trips west he visited her. He recalled one day in particular when they set out together to sketch on the waterfront below Beacon Hill across Marine Drive, the little woman not much higher than his knees. "There was a raven on her shoulder and I had a monkey by the hand…. She plunged into the traffic. I thought – there goes Emily Carr – in more ways than one." In 1945, Emily Carr died, leaving a magnificent heritage of distinctly Canadian creativity.

Every summer after 1951, Lismer and his wife set out by train for Vancouver, for they enjoyed the five-day isolation from the world. From Vancouver they took the ferry across to Nanaimo, a taxi to Port Alberni, a supply boat to the town of Ucluelet and a taxi to an inn on Wickaninnish Bay, the tongue-twister of a place that Lismer soon clarified to "Wicked Spinach." There they lived quietly.

The great Pacific where the gray whales lolloped through the waves was before them and the great forest behind. It was the forest that impelled Lismer this time. Here the great boles thrust their mighty height straight up and the sunlight slanted through the brood of giant trees. There was not the same struggle with the elements that had fascinated him in Georgian and McGregor bays.

He painted *Another Part of the Forest* with a great shaft of light illuminating the forest floor and thrusting the tree trunks into prominence. It was a timeless and often-used device, but in Lismer's development it was totally different from the thin rays that pierced the poplars that lined the road along which his Belgian refugees fled in 1915. It was different from the misty light that emanated from the heavens in *Old Pine, McGregor Bay*. This light was strong and sustaining. The brush strokes in this painting were as bold as ever, and the lush growth on the forest floor was scratched in with the end of his brush, a trick he had employed often before in his tangled Atlantic coast paintings. The yellow sunlight was scumbled with a diagonal swish of green to indicate a tree behind it. The heavy foliage of the branches appeared as a curtain bringing the top of the canvas into the picture. This was a device he had used before with clouds in *Evening Silhouette* (1926). All the tricks were old, but the setting was new. Arthur Lismer could still surprise.

He painted several versions of Lismer Bay, a little cove he loved. Fine details were left behind now, but the impression was strong. Although he made no attempt to match the mystique of Emily Carr, Lismer's paintings were nevertheless filled with the earth force, the vitality that was undeniably his mark. The colours of his palette were more restricted. Green predominated, for he was surrounded by the lush vegetation of the forest, and growth was the essence of the life Lismer loved.

Sometimes he would sketch with pencil or pen the details of leaf, stem, vine and bush that grew near. These sketches are informal, subtle, and full of feeling. With his still vigorous sense of humour, he called them his "myopic art." As he neared fourscore years, his hand shook a little, but when he took up his pencil or charcoal, the lines were as firm and strong as ever. Many fine grisailles comprise the output of his Vancouver summers.

He still valued his privacy in both Vancouver and Montreal, but he never withdrew from people. And he was still irrepressible, an elderly *enfant terrible*, a tradition refusing to become venerable. He would breeze into the Museum, pick up a child from some place, lift him to his shoulder and walk from picture to picture saying, "Now what do you think of this one?" or "Which one do you like best?" Or he would bend down to another who was bored waiting for his parents, "What did you expect to see when you came to an art gallery but haven't?" If the child said a giraffe, the famous artist would draw a giraffe or maybe a duck, for he was fond of ducks with their feisty stance.

Sometimes a child would initiate a friendship. "Did you see a fairy?" a three-year-old asked the tall man with a white fringe of hair and precarious eyeglasses. "Not this morning, but I'll draw one for you," answered seventy-four-year-old Dr Lismer. He crouched beside the little one and turned out a red pastel fairy.[3]

He would whirl into a classroom and the children would gather around him like flies. He would grab a piece of paper, whip a pencil or piece of charcoal out of his pocket, create a

Figure 98
A.J. Casson, Lawren Harris, Frederick Varley, A.Y. Jackson and Arthur Lismer at the Lawren Harris Exhibition, The Art Gallery of Toronto *1948*

Figure 99
CANADIAN ROCKIES (*from
the artist's sketchbook*) 1952
pencil on paper

sketch with a few strokes and be gone again, leaving a wave of wonder behind him.

He would often drop into the Sherbrooke Street art galleries. When a parent forgot a child while pondering an acquisition, she would rush in search of her, only to find Lismer feeding sugar lumps or candies to her offspring. "She may not remember this, but I will," the parent might say when she recognized the well-known face with its halo of hair.

This happy life in Montreal had been graced for some time with honours that were pouring in. His election to the Royal Canadian Academy in 1946 and to the council in 1951 were only two. He received an honourary LL.D from Dalhousie University, 1942; was made assistant professor in McGill University's newly established Department of Fine Arts, teaching the theory of design and the history of art, 1948; received the Greer Memorial Award from the Ontario Association of Teachers of Arts and Crafts, 1956; a Canada Council Medal, 1963; and another LL.D from McGill, 1963, an event that he celebrated by caricaturing himself in an academic gown using his mortarboard as a palette. The year 1967 brought twin honours: the Centennial Medal and Companion of the Order of Canada. Again he drew himself, this time with the medal resplendent on his chest, a quizzical expression on his face, a question mark rising from his pipe, and a characteristic pun on his signature – MEDAL.[4]

In 1955, yet another honour was accorded him. He became the first member of the Group of Seven to have his biography written. His friend, Dr John A.B. McLeish, Registrar of Carleton College at the time and former book critic for the Montreal *Gazette*, realized that Lismer's double career as teacher and artist had made him the most significant member of the Group of Seven. Lismer was pleased and a trifle flattered at the thought of being the subject of a book. In spite of his flamboyance and long sojourn in the public eye because of his principalships and lecture tours, he was a very private person who considered himself somewhat insignificant, because anything he had done seemed only what came naturally to him. He worked for causes, not for himself. Nevertheless, he cooperated with the project and fitted into his busy life as many sessions as he could with his biographer.

Figure 100
ROCKS, VANCOUVER
ISLAND 1960
brush and ink on paper
29.8 × 40 cm

Figure 101
BABES IN THE WOOD *n.d.*
charcoal on paper

Figure 102
TALL TREES *n.d.*
charcoal on paper
44.5 × 29.3 cm

Figure 103
EMILY CARR WITH HER
MONKEY AND DOGS 1933
charcoal, pen and black ink on
wove paper
18.4 × 23.5 cm

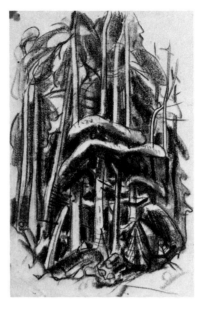

One day after he and McLeish had finished conferring, the two men went out for lunch at the Faculty Club. Lismer, in a rush as usual, started to cross the street without looking. McLeish pulled him back just as a truck missed him by inches.

"Thank you," said Arthur Lismer.

"You're welcome," said John McLeish. Then he added, "I don't know if I should have done that or not. You'd be a lot easier to handle dead than alive!"[5] That was one time when Lismer could not quip back.

He was still principal of the School of Art with his office in the Children's Art Centre. On February 24, 1960, an early morning fire in the Art Centre destroyed most of the interior of the building and the contents of his office. He did not regret the loss of about thirty of his sketches and one hundred drawings as much as the records pertaining to his long-time work with child art, his library and teaching materials. These were the records of his endeavours to shape the Montreal Museum of Fine Arts into "a breathing place for the spirit, as sustaining to the expansive and responsive nature as a cathedral and as beneficial."[6]

Now it was time to think of retiring. Whenever the subject came up Lismer scoffed, "Retire? Why my whole nature is retiring." Nevertheless, the inevitable came to pass. First he retired as professor of fine arts at McGill in 1955, at the age of

seventy. Then on June 30, 1967, he became Principal Emeritus of the School of Art at the Montreal Museum. It was a hard step to take and a hard word to pun. There was the customary farewell dinner and, with his usual flair and his most advanced calligraphic style, he sketched his version of it.

He was eighty-two years old. About his only concession to the new, more relaxed state was reading a few more detective stories than he had been able to before. His favourite authors were Chandler, Halliday, Latimer and Hammett. There were his usual spring visits with his daughter Marjorie, who had married Philip Bridges of New York in 1941 and moved with her family to Washington. There he entertained his three granddaughters, Barbara, Carolyn and Janet, with his puckish humour and drawings.

He rose as usual at seven o'clock, breakfasted on orange juice, roman meal (a stomach-filling habit acquired from Lawren Harris and the boxcar days in Algoma), toast and milk or tea with six sugar lumps in it. He walked swiftly out of the Fort Street apartment along Sherbrooke to the Museum. His hat, slightly battered, sat on the side of his head, his pipe was angled in his mouth, his scarf streamed behind and his coat flapped around his long legs like the clothes on an amiable scarecrow. He was a familiar and beloved figure to Montrealers.

It was inevitable now that the man who had been a one-man

Plate 37
ANOTHER PART OF THE
FOREST, B.C. 1952
oil on plywood
40.6 × 30.5 cm

Plate 38
SKUNK CABBAGE *n.d.*
oil on panel
30.5 × 40.6 cm

army in his endeavours was beginning to slow down. More than honours weighed on him now. The sugar lumps landed in his trouser cuffs as often as in his hand when he entertained a child. But he still surged along Sherbrooke Street to his beloved Museum as if his eyes were as clear as when he had looked through the embattled trees to the storm-lashed waves of Georgian Bay. His memory tricked him at times and the twinkle in his blue eyes was dimming. Laissez passer, but he still whisked away like one of the giddy ducks he had drawn so often. Soon after that he would whisk away no more.

On March 23, 1969, Arthur Lismer died. On March 25th, there was a private family funeral and on March 28th, a memorial service from the Unitarian Church at Simpson and Sherbrooke streets next to the Museum. On April 5, 1969, Arthur Lismer's ashes were the first to be interred in a knoll in the grounds of the McMichael Canadian Collection in Kleinburg, Ontario. A rose to symbolize England and a pine branch for Canada were laid there by his old friend, A.Y. Jackson. A.J. Casson gave the eulogy. Later, a great Algoma rock would mark the spot. In July 1976 his wife Esther joined him there.

Canada "is not a subtle country. The seasons succeed one another like bang! bang! bang!…and the sunsets come down with a thump," he had said years before when the beauty of new country burst upon him.[7] In the beautiful Ontario setting among his friends, there lies the artist and the educator, the legend in his own time, the man who said and lived the words: "The scientist can bring the faggots, but the artist brings the fire."

Figure 104
Penguins (sketch) *n.d.*
conté on paper
38.1 × 31.8 cm

Figure 105
SUMAC AT EVENTIDE,
GEORGIAN BAY 1950
oil on board
30.5 × 29.2 cm

Figure 106
Detail from the artist's sketchbook n.d.
ink on paper

NOTES

1 Pearl McCarthy, Toronto *Globe and Mail*, March 15, 1959
2 Edythe Hembroff Schleicher. *Emily Carr: The Untold Story.* (Saanichton, B.C., 1978) p. 84
3 Ken Johnstone, *New Liberty* (May 1951)
4 Marjorie Lismer Bridges. *A Border of Beauty.* Toronto: Red Rock Publishing Company Limited, 1977, p. 88
5 John McLeish to Lois Darroch, October 1980
6 Josephine Hambleton, Ottawa *Evening Citizen*, February 1, 1947
7 Betty Guernsey, *Montreal*, May–June 1968

Chronology

1885	Born June 27, Sheffield, England
1898 to 1905	Scholarship at the Sheffield School of Art
1899 to 1905	Apprenticed to photo-engraving company, Sheffield
1906	Travels to Antwerp to study at the Academie Royale des Beaux Arts
1908 to 1910	Works at commercial art studio in Sheffield
1911	*January* Travels from Liverpool, England to Halifax, Nova Scotia
	First employed by David Smith & Company in Toronto
	Later goes to Rapid Grip and Batten Company
1912	*May* Returns to England via New York
	July Marries Esther Ellen Mawson in Sheffield. Returns to Toronto
1913	Becomes Member of the Ontario Society of Artists (1913 to 1969)
	May Birth of daughter, Marjorie
	September First visit to Georgian Bay
1914	*May* First visit to Algonquin Park, with Thomson
1915	*Spring* Moves to Thornhill from Toronto
	Summer Appointed instructor in the Teachers Summer Course in Art, Ontario Department of Education. Holds same position the following summer
1916	Appointed Principal of the Victoria School of Art and Design, Halifax, Nova Scotia
1917	*December* Halifax explosion
1918	*June* Begins work for the Canadian War Records in Halifax
1919	*April* Appointment confirmed as Vice-Principal, Ontario College of Art
1920	*May* First Group of Seven show, Art Gallery of Toronto
1924	*August to September* Travels to England. Sees Wembley Exhibition
1926	*April* Appointed to Education Committee, Art Gallery of Toronto
	Publication of *Short History of Painting with a Note on Canadian Art*
1927	*June* Resigns from the Ontario College of Art
	September Appointed to the Art Gallery of Toronto to direct art education
1928	*Fall* Begins Saturday classes for children, Art Gallery of Toronto
1929	*Fall* Appointed Supervisor of Education, Art Gallery of Toronto
1932	*March and April* Western lecture tour for the National Gallery of Canada
	July to September Travels to Europe to Sixth World Conference of the New Education Fellowship. Then leads an "Art Appreciation" tour in Italy and France (last year with Teachers Summer Course)
1933	Founding member of the Canadian Group of Painters

October Opening of the Children's Art Centre, Art Gallery of Toronto

1934 *May to September* Travels to South Africa to the New Education Fellowship regional conferences in Cape Town and Johannesburg

1935 *July* Western lecture tour for the National Gallery of Canada

1936 Publication of *Education through Art for Children and Adults at the Art Gallery of Toronto*

1936 to 1937 *May to May* In South Africa, teaching and lecturing

1937 Travels to conferences of the New Education Fellowship in Australia and New Zealand
September Returns to Canada to resume work at the Art Gallery of Toronto

1938 *July* New Education Fellowship conference in Honolulu
August Resigns as Supervisor of Education, Art Gallery of Toronto
September Moves to New York as Visiting Professor of Fine Arts, Teachers College, Columbia University

1939 *August* Goes to Ottawa to direct education programs for the National Gallery of Canada

1940 *March* Lecture tour in the Maritimes for the National Gallery of Canada
April Lecture tour in the western provinces for the National Gallery of Canada
May Receives Honourary Diploma from the Nova Scotia College of Art (in absentia)
Resigns from National Gallery position

1941 Takes up appointment as Supervisor of Education, Montreal Art Association
June Kingston Conference, Federation of Canadian Artists
July Travels to Cranbrook and Ann Arbor, Michigan, for regional conferences of the Progressive Education Association
September Appointed Sessional Lecturer, School of Architecture, McGill University

1942 *May* Honourary LL.D from Dalhousie University, Halifax
Appointed Principal of the School of Art of the Montreal Art Association

1946 Opens Children's Art Centre, Montreal Art Association

1948 *September* Appointed Assistant Professor, Department of Fine Art, McGill University

1950 *January* Lismer Retrospective show opens in Toronto
February Elected Fellow of the Royal Society of Art, London, England

1952 *April* Film *Lismer* first shown at the Montreal Museum of Fine Arts

1953 University of Alberta National Award in Painting and Related Arts (in absentia)

1954 to 1955 President of the Canadian Group of Painters
and
1956 to 1957

1955 *November* Publication of *September Gale* by John A.B. McLeish
Retires from McGill University, age seventy

1956 Greer Memorial Award, presented by the Ontario Association of Teachers of Art

1963 *February* Canada Council Medal conferred
May Honourary LL.D from McGill University

1967 *June* 30 Retires as Principal of the School of Art and Design of the Montreal Museum of Fine Arts; designated Principal Emeritus
July 1 Centennial Medal
July 1 Companion of the Order of Canada announced, and conferred on November 24 in Ottawa

1969 *March* 23 Dies in Montreal
April Ashes buried in Kleinburg, at the McMichael Canadian Collection
Fall Posthumous award of Royal Canadian Academy of Arts Medal

Notes on Illustrations

Colour Plates

1. THE CANAL AT
DONCASTER 1906
watercolour over graphite on
wove paper
30 × 46 cm
s.l.r.: *A. Lismer 06*
National Gallery of Canada,
Ottawa

2. GEORGIAN BAY 1913
oil on canvas
71.8 × 92.1 cm
s.l.l.: *A. Lismer 1913*
National Gallery of Canada,
Ottawa
Gift of the Artist, Montreal, 1955
Photography: L.V. Cave,
Ottawa, 1970

3. AUTUMN IN
ALGONQUIN n.d.
oil on wood panel
20.4 × 26.4 cm
s.l.r.: *A. Lismer*
Mr and Mrs F. Schaeffer,
Toronto
Photography: VIDA/Saltmarche,
Toronto

4. UNTITLED (Belgian
refugees) 1915
gouache
45.7 × 58.4 cm
s.l.r.: *A. Lismer 15*
Private Collection
Photography: Tom Moore

5. SPRINGTIME ON THE
FARM c.1917
oil on canvas
30.4 × 40.6 cm
s.l.l.: *A. Lismer 17*
Montreal Museum of Fine Arts,
Montreal
Gift of the A. Sidney Dawes
Fund

6. POPPIES, BEDFORD
PARK AVENUE 1924
oil on board
66 × 81.3 cm
s.l.r.: *A. LISMER*
Private Collection

7. THE RIVER DRIVERS, n.d.
oil on panel
22.9 × 39.5 cm
unsigned
Mr and Mrs Walter H. Klinkhoff, Montreal
Photography: Notman and Son

8. WINTER CAMOUFLAGE 1918
oil on canvas
71.1 × 91.4 cm
s.l.r.: *A. LISMER 18*
National Gallery of Canada,
Ottawa

9. CONVOY AT SEA 1920
oil on canvas
163.2 × 213.3 cm
s.l.l.: *A. Lismer 1920*
Norman MacKenzie Art Gal-
lery, Regina
Gift of the Regina Boat Club

10. RAIN IN THE NORTH
COUNTRY c. 1920
oil on panel
22.3 × 30 cm
s.l.l.: *LISMER*
The McMichael Canadian Collection, Kleinburg

11. ISLES OF SPRUCE 1922
oil on canvas
119.4 × 162.6 cm
s.l.l.: *A. LISMER 22*
Hart House Permanent Collection, Hart House
University of Toronto, Toronto
Photography: Powey Chang,
Art Gallery of Ontario

12. A SEPTEMBER GALE,
GEORGIAN BAY 1921
oil on canvas
121.9 × 162.6 cm
s.l.r.: *A. Lismer 21*
National Gallery of Canada,
Ottawa

13. GEORGIAN BAY C.1925
oil on panel
30 × 40.6 cm
s.l.l.: *A. Lismer.*
Private Collection
Photography: VIDA/Saltmarche,

14. QUEBEC VILLAGE 1926
oil on canvas
132.1 × 162.6 cm
s.l.l.: *A. LISMER 26*
The Agnes Etherington Arts
Centre, Kingston
Gift of H.S. Southam, 1949

15. THE MILL, QUEBEC 1925
oil on canvas
82 × 102.2 cm
s.l.l.: *A. Lismer 25*
National Gallery of Canada,
Ottawa

16. CATHEDRAL
MOUNTAIN 1928
oil on canvas
121.9 × 142.2 cm
s.l.r.: *A LISMER 28*
Montreal Museum of Fine Arts,
Montreal
Gift of the A. Sidney Dawes
Fund

17. SUNLIGHT IN A
WOOD 1930
oil on canvas
91.4 × 101.6 cm
s.l.l.: *A Lismer 30*
Art Gallery of Ontario, Toronto
Bequest of John M. Lyle, 1946
Photography: Larry Ostrom, Art
Gallery of Ontario

18. BAIE ST PAUL,
QUEBEC 1931
oil on canvas
66 × 81.2 cm
s.l.r.: *A. Lismer 31*
Power Corporation of Canada,
Montreal
Photography: Notman and Son

19. GLACIER ABOVE
MORAINE LAKE 1926
oil on canvas
101.5 × 126.7 cm
s.l.r.: *AL*
The Art Gallery of Hamilton,
Hamilton
Gift of the Women's Committee,
1960

20. SOMBRE ISLE OF PIC,
LAKE SUPERIOR C. 1927
oil on canvas
86.4 × 110.5 cm
s.l.r.: *A LISMER*
The Winnipeg Art Gallery,
Winnipeg

21. BRIGHT LAND 1938
oil on canvas
81.1 × 101.5 cm
s.l.l.: *A. Lismer 38*
The McMichael Canadian
Collection, Kleinburg

22. PINE RHYTHM 1947
oil on canvas
53.3 × 66 cm
s.l.r.: *A Lismer 47*
Private Collection
Photography: Notman and Son

23. ROCKY CHANNEL,
MACGREGOR BAY 1935
oil on board
54.6 × 66 cm
s.l.c.: *A. Lismer 35*
Private Collection
Photography: Notman and Son

24. LITTLE LAKE, BAIE
FINN 1932
oil on canvas
66.7 × 81.5 cm
s.l.l.: *A. Lismer*
The Art Gallery of Hamilton,
Hamilton
Bequest of H.S. Southam, Esq.,
C.M.G., LL.D, 1966

25. PINE WRACK 1933
oil on canvas
92.1 × 106.9 cm
s.l.r.: *A. Lismer' 33*
The National Gallery of Canada, Ottawa
The Royal Canadian Academy,
diploma work, deposited 1948

26. DOCK LITTER C.1940
oil on canvas mounted on wood
40.6 × 50.8 cm
unsigned
Permanent Collection, Sarnia
Public Library and Art Gallery,
Sarnia

27. FISHING GEAR, CAPE
BRETON ISLAND 1940
watercolour on paper
30.5 × 45.7 cm
s.l.l.: *Arthur Lismer 1940*
s.l.r.: *Ingonish*
Art Gallery of Ontario, Toronto
Photography: Powey Chang,
Art Gallery of Ontario

28. CAPE BRETON, NOVA
SCOTIA, NEAR
CHETICAMP 1939
oil on plywood
61. × 81.2 cm
s.l.l.: *A. Lismer 39*
Kaspar Gallery, Toronto
Photography: Tom Moore

29. THE BIG ROCK, BON
ECHO 1922
oil on canvas
91.6 × 101.7 cm
s.l.r.: *A. Lismer 22*
National Gallery of Canada,
Ottawa

30. THE BOAT DECK 1933
oil on canvas
63.5 × 76.2 cm
s.l.c.: *A Lismer 33*
Private Collection

31. FALSE BAY, CAPE OF
GOOD HOPE 1938
graphite and watercolour on
paper
39 × 57.9 cm
s.l.r.: *A. LISMER. 38.*
National Gallery of Canada,
Ottawa
Gift of the Artist, Montreal,
1955

32. MOCHUDI, BECHUANA
VILLAGE 1936
oil on panel
31 × 40 cm
s.l.l: *A. Lismer 36*
National Gallery of Canada,
Ottawa

33. POTS OF FLOWERS 1938
watercolour
33 × 50.8 cm
s.l.l: *A. Lismer 38*
Rodman Hall Arts Centre,
St Catharines
Gift of Mr and Mrs C.S. Band,
in memory of Mrs C.M. Hill,
1964
Photography: VIDA/Saltmarche,
Toronto

34. THE BLUE BOAT,
NEIL'S HARBOUR, CAPE
BRETON 1945
oil on board
50.8 × 61 cm
s.l.l.: *A. Lismer 45*
Private Collection
Photography: Notman and Son

35. SEA SHELLS, N.S. C.1932
oil on panel
15.9 × 22.9 cm
s.l.l.: *A. Lismer*
Private Collection
Photography: Notman and Son

36. STILL LIFE 1951
oil on canvas
54.9 × 76.5 cm
s.l.l.: *A. Lismer 51*
Montreal Museum of Fine Arts,
Montreal

37. ANOTHER PART OF
THE FOREST, B.C. 1952
oil on plywood
40.6 × 30.5 cm
s.l.r.: *A LISMER*
Kaspar Galleries, Toronto
Photography: Tom Moore

38. SKUNK CABBAGE n.d.
oil on panel
30.5 × 40.6 cm
s.l.l.: *A LISMER*
Mr and Mrs Walter H. Klinkhoff, Montreal
Photography: Notman and Son

Black and White Illustrations

1. *King and Yonge Streets,
Toronto* c.1911
Courtesy of the City of Toronto
Archives

2. *7 Raven Road, Sheffield,
England*
Private Collection

3. *Edward and Harriet Lismer,
Arthur's parents*
Private Collection

4. *The Heeley Art Club*
Courtesy of the Graves Art Gallery, Sheffield

5. *Arthur Lismer and his sister
Constance*
Private Collection

6 – 10. *Sketches from the artist's
Sheffield period*
Graves Art Gallery, Sheffield

11. *Arthur Lismer's farewell
card from the Heeley Art Club*
Graves Art Gallery, Sheffield

12. *A view of Georgian Bay*
Courtesy of the Ontario Minis-
try of Natural Resources, Parks
and Recreational Areas Branch,
Toronto

13. *Albert Robson, art director
at "The Grip"*
The McMichael Canadian
Collection, Kleinburg
Photography: Tom Moore

14. *306 Delaware Avenue,
Toronto*
Private Collection

15. THE BANKS OF THE
DON c.1912
oil on panel
13.7 × 22 cm
s.l.l.: *A. Lismer*
National Gallery of Canada,
Ottawa
Bequest of Dr J.M. MacCallum,
Toronto, 1944

16. *Dr James MacCallum*
c.1915
Courtesy of the National
Gallery of Canada, Ottawa

17. GEORGIAN BAY
ISLANDS c.1921
pencil on paper
28.8 × 39.7 cm
s.l.l.: *AL*
The McMichael Canadian
Collection, Kleinburg
Photography: Tom Moore

18. *Algonquin Park*
Courtesy of the Ontario Minis-
try of Natural Resources, Parks
and Recreational Areas Branch,
Toronto

19. *Arthur Lismer*
Courtesy of the National
Gallery of Canada, Ottawa

20. TOM THOMSON c.1914
pencil on cardboard
26.4 × 33.4 cm
unsigned
The McMichael Canadian
Collection, Kleinburg
Photography: Tom Moore

21. THE GUIDE'S HOME,
ALGONQUIN 1914
oil on canvas
100.3 × 113 cm
s.l.l.: *A. Lismer/14*
National Gallery of Canada,
Ottawa

22. *Eric Brown, first director of
the National Gallery of Canada*
Courtesy of the National
Gallery of Canada, Ottawa

23. WOOD INTERIOR,
ALGONQUIN PARK 1914
oil on panel
23.2 × 31 cm
unsigned
National Gallery of Canada,
Ottawa
Bequest of Dr J.M.
MacCallum, Toronto, 1944

24. *121 Centre Street, Thornhill*
Courtesy of the Toronto *Star*,
Toronto

25. *Arthur Lismer with his wife
Esther and daughter Marjorie in
Algonquin Park*
Private Collection

26–31. THE MACCALLUM
MURALS 1915–16
oil on beaverboard
National Gallery of Canada,
Ottawa
Gift of Mr and Mrs H.R. Jack-
man, Toronto, 1967

32. *Lawren Harris* c.1917
Courtesy of the McMichael
Canadian Collection, Kleinburg
Photography: Tom Moore

33. *Patrol Boats, Dartmouth,
Nova Scotia* 1917
Courtesy of the Maritime
Command Museum, Halifax

34. *Marjorie in front of house in
Bedford, Nova Scotia*
Private Collection

35. THE LITTLE DRIFTER
AND THE BIG FREIGHTER
c.1919
lithograph
32.4 × 43.8 cm
unsigned
Canadian War Museum,
National Museum of Man,
National Museums of Canada,
Ottawa

36. STERN OF A DEPARTING
TRANSPORT 1917–18
lithograph
40.8 × 32.7 cm
s.l.r.: *A. Lismer*
Art Gallery of Ontario, Toronto
Gift of the Artist, 1926
Photography: Art Gallery of
Ontario

37. *The Halifax explosion*
Courtesy of the Halifax
Command Museum, Halifax

38. CONVOY IN BEDFORD
BASIN n.d.
oil on canvas
91.4 × 259 cm
Canadian War Museum,
National Museum of Man
National Museums of Canada,
Ottawa

39. MURALS PAINTED BY
ARTHUR LISMER IN THE
GREEN LANTERN
RESTAURANT, HALIFAX 1917
(restaurant destroyed by fire)
Courtesy of the National
Gallery of Canada, Ottawa
Original photograph: Private
Collection

40. *Sketch from the artist's
notebook of Marjorie having her
hair cut*
charcoal on paper
Private Collection

41–42. *Sketches from the
artist's Georgian Bay – Halifax
notebook*
Private Collection

43. *Arthur Lismer with
Marjorie*
Private Collection

44. *Sketch of Esther Lismer
reading*
charcoal on paper
Private Collection

45. *Self-portrait from the
artist's sketchbook*
charcoal on paper
Lois E. Darroch

46. HALIFAX HARBOUR,
TIME OF WAR c. 1917
oil on canvas
104.1 × 132.4 cm
s.l.r.: *A. Lismer*
Dalhousie Art Gallery, Halifax

47. ARRIVAL OF HOSPITAL
SHIP, PIER #2,
HALIFAX n.d.
lithograph
30 × 54 cm
s.l.l.: *AL*
s.l.r.: *Arthur Lismer*
Canadian War Museum,
National Museum of Man,
National Museums of Canada,
Ottawa

48. THE SENTINELS n.d.
lithograph on wove paper
53.5 × 39.5 cm
s.l.r.: *A. Lismer*
Canadian War Museum,
National Museum of Man,
National Museums of Canada,
Ottawa

49. A.Y. JACKSON (sketch
from artist's notebook) 1918
pencil on paper
25.4 × 19.9 cm
s.l.r.: *AL Halifax 1918*
Canadian War Museum,
National Museum of Man,
National Museums of Canada,
Ottawa

50. *Marjorie and Esther Lismer
on the day the* AQUITANIA
returned, Halifax
Private Collection

51. *Arthur Lismer*
Courtesy of the National
Gallery of Canada, Ottawa

52. *Lake Superior*
Courtesy of the Ontario Minis-
try of Natural Resources, Parks
and Recreational Areas Branch,
Toronto

53. *69 Bedford Park Avenue,
Toronto*
Private Collection

54. *Arthur Lismer's studio on
Bedford Park Avenue*
Private Collection

55. IN MY STUDIO 1924
oil on canvas
90.8 × 76.2 cm
s.l.r.: *A. Lismer*
The McMichael Canadian
Collection, Kleinburg

56. *Bertram Brooker, A.Y.
Jackson, Merrill Denison, J.E.H.
MacDonald, Lawren Harris,
Fred Housser and Arthur Lismer
at the Arts and Letters Club,
Toronto*
Courtesy of the Arts and Letters
Club of Toronto

57. *A.Y. Jackson, Frank Johnston and Lawren Harris on
the "Algoma Boxcar"*
Courtesy of the McMichael
Canadian Collection, Kleinburg

58. SAND LAKE, ALGOMA
c.1921
pencil on paper
20.6 × 28.6 cm
s.l.r.: *AL*
The McMichael Canadian
Collection, Kleinburg

59. ISLANDS OF
SPRUCE 1924–25
pen and ink on wove paper
27.8 × 35.6 cm
s.l.r.: *A.L.*
National Gallery of Canada,
Ottawa

60. GEORGIAN BAY 1926
brush and ink on paper
27.9 × 38.1 cm
s.l.l.: *A. Lismer 26*
Art Gallery of Ontario, Toronto
Photography: Art Gallery of
Ontario, Toronto

61. EVENING
SILHOUETTE 1928
oil on canvas
80.3 × 100.8 cm
s.l.r.: *A. LISMER*
University College, University
of Toronto, Toronto
H.S. Southam Bequest
Photography: Art Gallery of
Ontario, Toronto

62. PORTRAIT OF ERIC
BROWN c.1939
charcoal on wove paper
25.5 × 20.4 cm
unsigned
National Gallery of Canada,
Ottawa
Gift of Mrs Eric Brown,
Ottawa 1970
Photography: Michael Neill,
Ottawa, April 1978

63. STUDY FOR CATHEDRAL
MOUNTAIN c.1928
black chalk with white highlights
on green paper
unsigned
Montreal Museum of Fine Arts,
Montreal
Gift of Mrs Philip N. Bridges
(daughter of the artist)

64. *The Ontario College of Art,*
1924
Courtesy of the Ontario
College of Art, Toronto

65. SUNLIGHT IN A WOOD
(sketch) 1929
crayon on paper
27.9 × 37.8 cm
s.l.r.: *A. LISMER 29*
Art Gallery of Ontario, Toronto
Gift of the artist, 1946
Photography: Art Gallery of
Ontario

66. *The class at the Ontario*
College of Art c.1928 *(including*
Roy Mitchell, A.Y. Jackson,
Yvonne McKague Housser, J.W.
Beatty, Emanuel Hahn, Arthur
Lismer)
Courtesy of the Ontario
College of Art, Toronto

67. LISMER WITH LADIES
IN ART CLASS n.d.
charcoal on paper
12.7 × 19.3 cm
unsigned
The McMichael Canadian
Collection, Kleinburg
Photography: Tom Moore

68. *Class in progress at the*
Ontario College of Art
Courtesy of the Ontario College
of Art, Toronto

69. *Arthur Lismer and Madge*
Gough at the Beaux Arts Ball,
the Ontario College of Art
Courtesy of the Ontario
College of Art, Toronto

70. SAMMY SUMAC n.d.
pencil and oil pastel on paper
16.5 × 16.5 cm
unsigned
Montreal Museum of Fine Arts,
Montreal
Gift of Mrs Philip N. Bridges
(daughter of the artist) and Mrs
Arthur Lismer

71. *Saturday morning class in*
progress at the Art Gallery of
Toronto 1936
Courtesy of the Art Gallery of
Ontario, Toronto

72. *Humberside Collegiate,*
Toronto c.1928
Courtesy of the Toronto Board
of Education, Toronto

73. *The "allegorical" panel of*
the Humberside mural
Courtesy of Humberside
Collegiate, Toronto

74. *The La Cloche Mountains,*
Killarney
Courtesy of the Ontario Minis-
try of Natural Resources, Parks
and Recreational Areas Branch,
Toronto

75. FRANK CARMICHAEL n.d.
pencil on paper
19.6 × 25.1 cm
unsigned
The McMichael Canadian
Collection, Kleinburg
Photography: Tom Moore

76. BRIGHT LAND (*sketch*)
oil on board
45.7 × 54.5 cm
s.l.l.: *A LISMER*
Private Collection

77. LILIES AND APPLES 1931
oil on cardboard
30.7 × 40.5 cm
s.l.l.: *A Lismer 31*
National Gallery of Canada,
Ottawa
Photography: Saltmarche
Brothers, Toronto, 1978

78. MACGREGOR BAY 1933
ink on paper
30.5 × 38.1 cm
s.l.r.: *A. Lismer, MacGregor*
Bay. 1933
R. Merlo, Montreal

79. GEORGIAN BAY
PINE n.d.
pen and ink on paper
22.9 × 17. 8 cm
s.l.r.: *AL*
Mr and Mrs F. Schaeffer,
Toronto

80. *A South African landscape*
Courtesy of the South African
Tourist Corporation, Toronto

81. HARBOUR SCENE 1930
ink and watercolour
35.6 × 44.5 cm
s.l.l.: *A. Lismer*
Manuge Galleries Limited,
Halifax

82. DERELICT PIER 1941
oil on canvas
55.3 × 66 cm
unsigned
Art Gallery of Ontario, Toronto
Gift from the Albert H. Robson
Memorial Subscription Fund,
1942
Photography: Art Gallery of
Ontario

83. ROCKY HARBOUR n.d.
ink on paper
26.6 × 37.2 cm
unsigned
The McMichael Canadian
Collection, Kleinburg
Photography: Tom Moore

84. BARN, ILE
D'ORLEANS 1925
reed-pen and black ink
31.8 × 37.3 cm
s.l.l.: *A LISMER 25*
National Gallery of Canada,
Ottawa

85. ON THE GATINEAU 1926
brush and ink on paper
27.9 × 38.1 cm
s.l.r.: *A Lismer 26*
s.l.l.: *On the Gatineau*
Art Gallery of Ontario, Toronto
Photography: Art Gallery of
Ontario, Toronto

86. AFRICAN HUT, SOUTH
AFRICA C.1935
charcoal on paper
21.5 × 33 cm
s.l.r.: *AL*
The McMichael Canadian
Collection, Kleinburg
Photography: Tom Moore

87. SKETCH OF
ELEPHANTS, PENGUINS,
MONKEYS AND BIRDS n.d.
ink drawing
16.3 × 13 cm
unsigned
Montreal Museum of Fine Arts,
Montreal
Gift of Mrs Philip N. Bridges
(daughter of the artist)

88. *Montreal* 1941
Courtesy of the Notman Photo-
graphic Archives, Montreal

89. *Arthur Lismer with students
at the Children's Art Centre,
Montreal*
Private Collection

90. CAR, GULL, FISH,
DIVER n.d.
watercolour
26.6 × 16.5 cm
unsigned
Montreal Museum of Fine Arts,
Montreal
Gift of Mrs Philip N. Bridges
(daughter of the artist)

91. INGONISH 1945
drybrush and ink on paper
43.8 × 58.7 cm
s.l.r.: *Arthur Lismer,
Ingonish./45*
Jennings Young, Toronto
Photography: VIDA/Saltmarche,
Toronto

92. KILLICK PARADE 1945
brush and ink on paper
29.8 × 45.7 cm
s.l.r.: *A Lismer 1945
     Neil's Harbour*, C.B.I.
Art Gallery of Ontario, Toronto
Photography: Art Gallery of
Ontario

93. BEACH STUDIES I (from
the artist's sketchbook) c.1951
charcoal on paper
22.4 × 29.8 cm
s.l.r.: *AL*
Art Gallery of Ontario,
Toronto
Gift of Marjorie Lismer Bridges
(daughter of the artist)
Photography: Art Gallery of
Ontario

94. *Arthur Lismer in his office
at the Montreal Museum of Fine
Arts, Montreal*
Private Collection

95. *Lismer Bay, Vancouver
Island*
Private Collection

96. *Arthur Lismer in front of
self-portrait*
Courtesy of the Art Gallery of
Ontario, Toronto

97. *Arthur Lismer speaking to
guests at his retrospective in 1950
at the Art Gallery of Toronto*
Courtesy of the Art Gallery of
Ontario, Toronto

98. *A.J. Casson, Lawren Harris,
Frederick Varley, A.Y. Jackson
and Arthur Lismer at the Law-
ren Harris Exhibition, The Art
Gallery of Toronto, 1948*
Courtesy of the Art Gallery of
Ontario, Toronto

99. CANADIAN ROCKIES
(from the artist's
sketchbook) 1952
pencil on paper
unsigned
Private Collection

100. ROCKS, VANCOUVER
ISLAND 1960
brush and ink on paper
29.8 × 40 cm
s.l.l.: *A. Lismer*
Art Gallery of Windsor
Collection, Windsor
Gift of the Director's Fund,
1962
Photography: Saltmarche,
Toronto

101. BABES IN THE
WOOD n.d.
charcoal on paper
s.l.l. *AL
     Babes in the Wood*
Private Collection

102. TALL TREES n.d.
charcoal on paper
44.5 × 29.3 cm
unsigned
The McMichael Canadian
Collection, Kleinburg
Photography: Tom Moore

103. EMILY CARR WITH
HER MONKEY AND
DOGS 1933
charcoal, pen and black ink on
wove paper
18.4 × 23.5 cm
s.l.l.: *A.L. 1933*
National Gallery of Canada,
Ottawa
Gift of the Artist, Montreal,
1960

104. *Penguins (sketch)* n.d.
conté on paper
38.1 × 31.8 cm
s.l.l.: *AL*
Doris Huestis Mills Speirs,
Pickering

105. SUMAC AT EVENTIDE,
GEORGIAN BAY 1950
oil on board
30.5 × 29.2 cm
s.l.c.: *AL*
Mrs Henry Jackman, Toronto

106. *Detail from the artist's
sketchbook* n.d.
ink on paper
Private Collection

Selected Bibliography

BARBEAU, MARIUS. *Folk Songs of Old Quebec*. Ottawa: National Museums of Canada. Bulletin no. 75, 1964 (illustrated by A. Lismer)

BRIDLE, AUGUSTUS. *The Story of the Club*. Toronto: The Arts and Letters Club, 1945

BROWN, F. MAUD. *Breaking Barriers: Eric Brown and the National Gallery*. Toronto: Society for Art Publications, 1964

Canadian Drawings: A Portfolio of Prints. Toronto: Rous and Mann Press, 1925

CARR, EMILY. *Hundreds and Thousands*. Toronto: Clarke, Irwin & Company Limited, 1966

Coasts, the Sea, and Canadian Art. Stratford: The Gallery, 1978

DUVAL, PAUL. *Canadian Drawings and Prints*. Toronto: Burns and MacEachern, 1952

DUVAL, PAUL. *Group of Seven Drawings*. Toronto: Burns and MacEachern, 1965

DUVAL, PAUL. *The Tangled Garden: The Art of J.E.H. MacDonald*. Toronto: Cerebrus/Prentice-Hall, 1978

GROVES, NAOMI JACKSON. *A.Y.'s Canada*. Toronto: Clarke, Irwin & Company Limited, 1968

HARRIS, BESS and COLGROVE, R.G.P., editors, Introduction by Northrop Frye. *Lawren Harris*. Toronto: Macmillan Company, 1969

HARRIS, LAWREN. *Lismer Paintings, 1913–1949*. Toronto: Art Gallery of Toronto, 1950

HARRIS, LAWREN. *The Story of the Group of Seven*. Toronto: Rous and Mann Press, 1964

HOUSSER, F.B. *A Canadian Art Movement*. Toronto: Macmillan Company, 1926

HUBBARD, R.H. *Canadian Landscape Paintings: 1670–1930*. Madison, Wisconsin: Elvehjem Art Center, 1973

HUNKIN, HARRY. *There is no Finality...A Story of the Group of Seven*. Toronto: Burns and MacEachern, 1971

JACKSON, A.Y. *A Painter's Country*. Toronto: Clarke, Irwin & Company Limited, 1958

LAING, BLAIR. *Memoirs of An Art Dealer*. Toronto: McClelland and Stewart, 1979

LORD, BARRY. *The History of Painting in Canada: Toward a people's art*. Toronto: NC Press, 1974

MACDONALD, COLIN S. *A Dictionary of Canadian Artists*. Ottawa: Canadian Paperbacks, 1967 ff

MACDONALD, THOREAU. *The Group of Seven*. Canadian Art Series. Toronto: Ryerson Press, 1944

MCINNES, GRAHAM. *A Short History of Canadian Art*. Toronto: Macmillan Company, 1939

MCLEISH, JOHN A.B. *September Gale: A Study of Arthur Lismer*. Toronto: J.M. Dent and Sons Limited, 1955

MELLEN, PETER. *The Group of Seven*. Toronto: McClelland and Stewart Limited, 1970

MORRIS, JERROLD. *One Hundred Years of Canadian Drawings*. Toronto: Methuen Publications, 1980

MURRAY, JOAN. *Impressionism in Canada, 1895–1935*. Toronto: Art Gallery of Ontario, 1974

MURRAY, JOAN. *The Art of Tom Thomson*. Toronto: Art Gallery of Ontario, 1971

REID, DENNIS. *A Bibliography of the Group of Seven*. Ottawa: National Gallery of Canada, 1971

REID, DENNIS. *The MacCallum Bequest, of paintings by Tom Thomson and other Canadian Painters and the Mr. & Mrs. H.R. Jackman Gift of the Murals from the late Dr. MacCallum's cottage painted by some members of the Group of Seven*. Ottawa: National Gallery of Canada, 1969

REID, DENNIS. *The Group of Seven*. Exhibition. Ottawa: National Gallery of Canada, 1970

ROBSON, A.H. *Canadian Landscape Painters*. Toronto: Ryerson Press, 1932

The Group of Seven: Catalogue Exhibition of Paintings, May 7–27, 1920 ... Reconstruction, May 1–31, 1970. Toronto: Art Gallery of Ontario, 1970

TIPPETT, MARIA. *Emily Carr: A Biography*. Toronto: Oxford University Press, 1979

TOWN, HAROLD and SILCOX, DAVID P. *Tom Thomson: The Silence and the Storm*. Toronto: McClelland and Stewart, 1977

YANOVER, SHIRLEY. *The Gallery School 1930–1980: A Celebration*. Toronto: Art Gallery of Ontario, 1980

Selected Articles

AYRE, ROBERT. "Arthur Lismer." *Canadian Art*, IV, no. 2 (1947), 48–51

BALLANTYNE, MICHAEL. "Childhood and the World of Art." *Canadian Art*, XXI, no. 6 (November/December 1964), 336–341

BELL, ANDREW. "Lismer's Painting from 1913 to 1949 in Review." *Canadian Art*, VII, no. 3 (1950), 91–93

BRESLIN, CATHY. "A Canadian Art Master Meets and Teaches a New Generation." *Maclean's Magazine*, May 7, 1960

DUVAL, PAUL. "A Fascinating Evolution Seen in Lismer Exhibit." *Saturday Night*, February 16, 1946

FAIRLEY, BARKER. "The Group of Seven." *Canadian Forum*, V, no. 53 (February 1925), 144–147

FRYE, HELEN. "Arthur Lismer." *Pioneers in Adult Education*. Ed. Helen Rouillard for the Canadian Association for Adult Education

FULFORD, ROBERT. "They Started the New Look in Canadian Art." *Star Weekly*, April 23, 1960

HUNTER, E.R. "Arthur Lismer." *Maritime Art*, July–August 1943, 137–141, 168–169

JACKSON, A.Y. "Arthur Lismer: His Contribution to Canadian Art." *Canadian Art*, VII, no. 3 (1950), 89–90

JOHNSTONE, KEN. "The Professor is a Rebel." *New Liberty*, May, 1951, 32–33, 44–52

LORD, BARRY. "Georgian Bay and the Development of the September Gale Theme in Arthur Lismer's Painting, 1912–1921." *National Gallery of Canada Bulletin*, V, nos. 1, 2 (1967), 28–38

MACDONALD, J.E.H. "The Canadian Spirit in Art." *The Statesman*, II, no. 35 (1919), 6–7

MCCULLOUGH, NORAH. "The Art Centre: A Flourishing Plant." *Canadian Art*, IV, no. 1 (1946), 27–31

SALINGER, J.B. "Comment on Art: The Group of Seven." *Canadian Forum*, XII, no. 136 (1932), 142–143

Selected Bibliography: Arthur Lismer's Works

"Art in a Changing World." *Proceedings of the New Education Fellowship Conference, Modern Trends in Education*. Wellington, New Zealand, 1938

"Art a Common Necessity." *Canadian Bookman*, VII, no. 10 (1925), 156–160

"Art in the Machine Age." *Canadian Comment*, April 1932

"Canadian Art." *Canadian Theosophist*, V, no. 12 (February 5, 1925), 177–179

Canadian Picture Study. Toronto: Art Gallery of Toronto, 1930

"The Canadian War Memorials." *The Rebel*, IV, no. 1 (October 1919), 40–42

"Child Art in Canada." *The Studio*, LXXIX, no. 625, 118–119

"Child Art, a Critical Review of Some Experiments and Achievements." *Canadian Art*, XIV, no. 3 (1957), 112–116

"Children and Art." *Canadian Forum*, XVI, no. 4 (1936), 12–15

"Education Through Art." *The New Era in Home and School*, December 1934, 232–237

Education Through Art for Children and Adults at the Art Gallery of Toronto. Toronto: privately printed, 1936

"Graphic Art." *Yearbook of Canadian Art*, 1913

"Mural Painting." *Journal of the Royal Architectural Institute of Canada*, X, no. 7 (1933), 127–135

A Short History of Painting with a Note on Canadian Art. Toronto: Andrews Bros., 1926

"The Value, Meaning and Place of Art in Education." *Dalhousie Review*, October 1928, 378–389

"What is Child Art?" *Canadian Art*, V, no. 4 (1948), 178–179

Index

DESIGN The Dragon's Eye Press
PRODUCTION Paula Chabanais Productions
TYPESETTING University of Toronto Press
FILM Graphic Litho-Plate Inc.
LITHOGRAPHY Matthews, Ingham and Lake Inc.
BINDING The Hunter Rose Company Limited
PAPER 100 lb. Warren's Patina Matte
BINDING MATERIAL Joanna Kennett
TYPEFACE Stempel Garamond